WORDS TO LIVE BY

WORDS TO LIVE BY

A Guide for the Merely Christian

C. S. Lewis

Edited by Paul F. Ford

HarperSanFrancisco

A Division of HarperCollins*Publishers*

HarperCollins books may be purchased for educational, business, or sales promotional use. For information please write: Special Markets Department, HarperCollins Publishers, 10 East 53rd Street, New York, NY 10022.

HarperCollins Web site: http://www.harpercollins.com

HarperCollins®, ▦ ®, and HarperSanFrancisco™ are trademarks of HarperCollins Publishers.

FIRST EDITION

Library of Congress Cataloging-in-Publication Data is available upon request.
ISBN: 978–0–06–120912–3
ISBN-10: 0–06–120912–0

07 08 09 10 11 RRD(H) 10 9 8 7 6 5 4 3 2 1

EDITOR'S NOTE

We have retained Lewis's spellings and misspellings, abbreviations, and other idiosyncrasies. The principal abbreviations are:

&	and
C. of E.	Church of England
cd.	could
H.	Helen Joy Davidman Lewis
N.T.	New Testament
R.C.	Roman Catholic
shd.	should
tho'	(al)though
W.	Warren Hamilton Lewis
wd.	would
wh.	which
v.	very
Xtianity	Christianity
yr	your

Some references in *Words to Live By* are made to Lewis's use of the works of George MacDonald. In some ways, Lewis's *George MacDonald: An Anthology* is the key to understanding Lewis; no one can know Lewis until this book has been taken on board.

Paul F. Ford

ALMSGIVING

Charity—giving to the poor—is an essential part of Christian morality. . . . Some people nowadays say that charity ought to be unnecessary and that instead of giving to the poor we ought to be producing a society in which there were no poor to give to. They may be quite right in saying that we ought to produce that kind of society. But if anyone thinks that, as a consequence, you can stop giving in the meantime, then he has parted company with all Christian morality. I do not believe one can settle how much we ought to give. I am afraid the only safe rule is to give more than we can spare.

Mere Christianity

On the duty of alms-giving, and even on the subtle corruptions of alms-giving, few men have written better than Calvin himself. The limit of giving is to be the limit of our ability to give. We must not consider ourselves free to refuse because those who ask us are <u>undeserving</u>, "for Scripture here cometh to our aide with this excellent reason, that we respect not what men merit of themselves but looke only upon God's image which they bear." We must guard against that subtle insolence which often poisons the gift. Even "a merry countenance and courteous wordes" accompanying it are not enough. A Christian must not give "as though he would binde his brother unto him by the benefit." When I use my hands to heal some other part of my body I lay the body under no obligation to the hands: and since we are all members of one another, we similarly lay no obligation on the poor when we relieve them *(Institutio,* III. vii. 6, 7).

English Literature in the Sixteenth Century Excluding Drama

ASCETICISM

To shrink back from all that can be called Nature into negative spirituality is as if we ran away from horses instead of learning to ride. There is in our present pilgrim condition plenty of room (more room than most of us like) for abstinence and renunciation and mortifying our natural desires. But behind all asceticism the thought should be, "Who will trust us with the true wealth if we cannot be trusted even with the wealth that perishes?" Who will trust me with a spiritual body if I cannot control even an earthly body? These small and perishable bodies we now have were given to us as ponies are given to schoolboys. We must learn to manage: not that we may some day be free of horses altogether but that some day we may ride bare-back, confident and rejoicing, those greater mounts, those winged, shining and world-shaking horses which perhaps even now expect us with impatience, pawing and snorting in the King's stables. Not that the gallop would be of any value unless it were a gallop with the King; but how else—since He has retained His own charger—should we accompany Him?

Miracles

Because God created the Natural—invented it out of His love and artistry—it demands our reverence; because it is only a creature and not He, it is, from another point of view, of little account. And still more, because Nature, and especially human nature, is fallen it must be corrected and the evil within it must be morti-

3

fied. But its essence is good; <u>correction</u> is something quite different from Manichaean <u>repudiation</u> or <u>Stoic superiority</u>. Hence, in
all true Christian asceticism, that respect for the thing rejected
which, I think, we never find in pagan asceticism. Marriage is
good, though not for me; wine is good, though I must not drink
it; feasts are good, though today we fast.

The wrong asceticism torments the self: the right kind kills
the selfness. We must die daily: but it is better to love the self
than to love nothing, and to pity the self than to pity no one.

God in the Dock

ASSURANCE

Sorry you're in a trough. I'm just emerging (at least I hope I am) from a long one myself. As for the difficulty of believing it is a trough, one wants to be careful about the word "believing." We too often mean by it "having confidence or assurance as a psychological state"—as we have about the existence of furniture. But that comes and goes and by no means always accompanies intellectual assent, e.g., in learning to swim you believe, and even know intellectually that water will support you long before you feel any real confidence in the fact. I suppose the perfection of faith wd. make this confidence invariably proportionate to the assent.

In the meantime, as one has learnt to swim only by acting on the assent in the teeth of all instinctive conviction, so we shall proceed to faith only by acting as if we had it. Adapting a passage in the Imitation one can say "What would I do now if I had a full assurance that there was only a temporary trough" and having got the answer, go and do it. I a man, therefore lazy: you a woman, therefore probably a fidget. So it may be good advice to you (though it wd. be bad to me) not even to try to do in the trough all you can do on the peak.

The Collected Letters of C. S. Lewis, Volume II

My primary field is the past. I travel with my back to the engine, and that makes it difficult when you try to steer. The world might stop in ten minutes; meanwhile, we are to go on doing our duty. The great thing is to be found at one's post as a child of God, living each day as though it were our last, but planning as though our world might last a hundred years.

We have, of course, the assurance of the New Testament regarding events to come. I find it difficult to keep from laughing when I find people worrying about future destruction of some kind or other. Didn't they know they were going to die anyway?

God in the Dock

BAPTISM

"It is well," said Mother Kirk. "You have come a long way round to reach this place, whither I would have carried you in a few moments. But it is very well."

"What must I do?" said John.

"You must take off your rags," said she, "as your friend has done already, and then you must dive into this water."

"Alas," said he, "I have never learned to dive."

"There is nothing to learn" said she. "The art of diving is not to do anything new but simply to cease doing something. You have only to let yourself go."

"It is only necessary," said Vertue, with a smile, "to abandon all efforts at self-preservation."

"I think," said John, "that if it is all one, I would rather jump."

"It is not all one," said Mother Kirk. "If you jump, you will be trying to save yourself and you may be hurt. As well, you would not go deep enough. You must dive so that you can go right down to the bottom of the pool: for you are not to come up again on this side. There is a tunnel in the cliff, far beneath the surface of the water, and it is through that that you must pass so that you may come up on the far side."

"I see," thought John to himself, "that they have brought me here to kill me," but he began, nevertheless, to take off his clothes. They were little loss to him, for they hung in shreds, plastered with blood and with the grime of every shire from Puritania to the canyon: but they were so stuck to him that they came away with pain and a little skin came with them. When he was naked, Mother Kirk bade him come to the edge of the pool, where Vertue was already standing. It was a long way down to the water, and the reflected moon seemed to look up at him from the depth of a mine. He had had some thought of throwing himself in, with a run, the very instant he reached the edge, before he had time to be afraid. And the making of that resolution had seemed to be itself the bitterness of death, so that he half believed the worst must be over and that he would find himself in the water before he knew. . . .

"Come on, John," [Vertue] said, "the longer we look at it the less we shall like it." And with that he took a header into the pool and they saw him no more. And how John managed it or what he felt I did not know, but he also rubbed his hands, shut his eyes, despaired, and let himself go. It was not a good dive, but, at least, he reached the water head first.

The Pilgrim's Regress

Don't bother at all about that question of a person being "made a Christian" by baptism. It is only the usual trouble about words being used in more than one sense. Thus we might say a man "became a soldier" the moment that he joined the army. But his instructors might say six months later "I think we have made a soldier of him." Both usages are quite definable, only one wants to know which is being used in a given sentence. The Bible itself gives us one short prayer which is suitable for all who are struggling with the beliefs and doctrines. It is: Lord, I believe, help Thou my unbelief.

The Collected Letters of C. S. Lewis, Volume III

BEAUTY

The beauty of the female is the root of joy to the female as well as to the male, and it is no accident that the goddess of Love is older and stronger than the god. To desire the desiring of her own beauty is the vanity of Lillith, but to desire the enjoying of her own beauty is the obedience of Eve, and to both it is in the lover that the beloved tastes her own delightfulness. . . .

For beauty was made for others. Her beauty belonged to the Director. It belonged to him so completely that he could even decide not to keep it for himself but to order that it be given to another, by an act of obedience lower, and therefore higher, more unconditional and therefore more delighting, than if he had demanded it for himself.

That Hideous Strength

We want so much more—something the books on aesthetics take little notice of. But the poets and the mythologies know all about it. We do not want merely to see beauty, though, God knows, even that is bounty enough. We want something else which can hardly be put into words—to be united with the beauty we see, to pass into it, to receive it into ourselves, to bathe in it, to become part of it.

The Weight of Glory

It was when I was happiest that I longed most . . . The sweetest thing in all my life has been the longing . . . to find the place where all the beauty came from.

Till We Have Faces

BIBLE

Unless the religious claims of the Bible are again acknowledged, its literary claims will, I think, be given only "mouth honour" and that decreasingly. . . . It is, if you like to put it that way, not merely a sacred book but a book so remorselessly and continuously sacred that it does not invite, it excludes or repels, the merely aesthetic approach. You can read it as literature only by a tour de force. You are cutting the wood against the grain, using the tool for a purpose it was not intended to serve. It demands incessantly to be taken on its own terms: it will not continue to give literary delight very long except to those who go to it for something quite different.

Selected Literary Essays

It is Christ Himself, not the Bible, who is the true word of God. The Bible, read in the right spirit and with the guidance of good teachers, will bring us to Him. When it becomes really necessary (i.e., for our spiritual life, not for controversy or curiosity) to know whether a particular passage is rightly translated or is Myth (but of course Myth specially chosen by God from among countless Myths to carry a spiritual truth) or history, we shall no doubt be guided to the right answer. But we must not use the Bible (our fathers too often did) as a sort of Encyclopedia out of which texts (isolated from their context and not read without attention to the whole nature & purport of the books in which they occur) can be taken for use as weapons. . . .

To me the curious thing is that neither in my own Bible-reading nor in my religious life as a whole does the question in fact even assume that importance which it always gets in theological controversy. The difference between reading the story of Ruth and that of Antigone—both first class as literature—is to me unmistakable and even overwhelming. But the question "Is Ruth historical?" (I've no reason to suppose it is not) doesn't really seem to arise till afterwards. It wd. still act on me as the Word of God if it weren't, so far as I can see. All Holy Scripture is written for our learning. But learning of what? I should have thought the value of some things (e.g., the Resurrection) depended on whether they really happened: but the value of others (e.g., the fate of Lot's wife) hardly at all. And the ones whose historicity matters are, as God's will, those where it is plain.

The Collected Letters of C. S. Lewis, Volume III

Whatever these men [modern biblical critics] may be as Biblical critics, I distrust them as critics. They seem to me to lack literary judgement, to be imperceptive about the very quality of the texts they are reading. It sounds a strange charge to bring against men who have been steeped in those books all their lives. But that might be just the trouble. A man who has spent his youth and manhood in the minute study of New Testament texts and of other people's studies of them, whose literary experiences of those texts lacks any standard of comparison such as can only grow from a wide and deep genial experience of literature in general, is, I should think, very likely to miss the obvious things about them. If he tells me that something in a Gospel is legend or romance, I want to know how many legends and romances he has read, how well his palate is trained in detecting them by the flavour; not how many years he has spent on that Gospel. . . .

These men ask me to believe they can read between the lines of the old texts; the evidence is their obvious inability to read (in any sense worth discussing) the lines themselves. They claim to see fern-seed and can't see an elephant ten yards away in broad daylight.

Christian Reflections

I suggest two rules for exegetics: (1) Never take the images literally. (2) When the purport of the images—what they say to our fear and hope and will and affections—seems to conflict with the theological abstractions, trust the purport of the images every time. For our abstract thinking is itself a tissue of analogies: a continual modelling of spiritual reality in legal or chemical or mechanical terms. Are these likely to be more adequate than the sensuous, organic, and personal images of Scripture—light and darkness, river and well, seed and harvest, master and servant, hen and chickens, father and child? The footprints of the Divine are more visible in that rich soil than across rocks or slag-heaps. Hence what they now call "demythologising" Christianity can easily be "re-mythologising" it—and substituting a poorer mythology for a richer.

Letters to Malcolm: Chiefly on Prayer

There is no such thing as translating a book into another language once and for all, for a language is a changing thing. If your son is to have clothes it is no good buying him a suit once and for all: he will grow out of it and have to be reclothed. . . .

We must sometimes get away from the Authorised Version, if for no other reason, simply because it is so beautiful and so solemn. Beauty exalts, but beauty also lulls. Early associations endear but they also confuse. Through that beautiful solemnity the transporting or horrifying realities of which the Book tells may come through to us blunted and disarmed, and we may only sigh with tranquil veneration when we ought to be burning with shame or struck dumb with terror or carried out of ourselves by ravishing hopes and adorations. Does the word "scourged" really come home to us like "flogged"? Does "mocked him" sting like "jeered at him"?

God in the Dock

BODY

Man has held three views of his body. First there is that of those
ascetic Pagans who called it the prison or the "tomb" of the soul,
and of Christians like Fisher to whom it was a "sack of dung,"
food for worms, filthy, shameful, a source of nothing but temptation to bad men and humiliation to good ones. Then there are the
Neo-Pagans (they seldom know Greek), the nudists and the sufferers from Dark Gods, to whom the body is glorious. But thirdly
we have the view which St. Francis expressed by calling his body
"Brother Ass." All three may be—I am not sure—defensible; but
give me St. Francis for my money.

The Four Loves

Not that you and I have now much reason to rejoice in having bodies! Like old automobiles, aren't they? where all sorts
of apparently different things keep going wrong, but what they
add up to is the plain fact that the machine is wearing out. Well,
it was not meant to last forever. Still, I have a kindly feeling
for the old rattle-trap. Through it God showed me that whole
side of His beauty which is embodied in colour, sound, smell
and size. No doubt it has often led me astray: but not half so
often, I suspect, as my soul has led it astray. For the spiritual
evils which we share with the devils (pride, spite) are far worse
than what we share with the beasts: and sensuality really arises
more from the imagination than from the appetites; which, if

left merely to their own animal strength, and not elaborated by our imagination, would be fairly easily managed.

The Collected Letters of C. S. Lewis, Volume III

Bless the body. Mine has led me into many scrapes, but I've led it into far more. If the imagination were obedient, the appetites would give us very little trouble. And from how much it has saved me! And but for our body one whole realm of God's glory—all that we receive through the senses—would go unpraised. For the beasts can't appreciate it and the angels are, I suppose, pure intelligences. They understand colours and tastes better than our greatest scientists; but have they retinas or palates? I fancy the "beauties of nature" are a secret God has shared with us alone. That may be one of the reasons why we were made—and why the resurrection of the body is an important doctrine.

Letters to Malcolm: Chiefly on Prayer

BOOKS

The great thing is to be always reading but not to get bored—treat it not like work, more as a vice! Your book bill ought to be your biggest extravagance.

C. S. Lewis at the Breakfast Table and Other Reminiscences

The meaning of a book is the series or systems of emotions, reflections, and attitudes produced by reading it. . . .

This product differs with different readers. . . . The ideally true or right meaning would be that shared . . . by the largest number of the best readers after repeated and careful readings over several generations, different periods, nationalities, moods, degrees of alertness, private pre-occupations, states of health, spirits, and the like cancelling one another out when . . . they cannot be fused so as to enrich one another.

C. S. Lewis on Stories

[Question:] "What books did most to shape your vocational attitude and your philosophy of life?"

[Lewis's Answer:]

1) *Phantastes,* by George MacDonald
2) *The Everlasting Man,* by G. K. Chesterton
3) The *Aeneid,* by Virgil
4) *The Temple,* by George Herbert
5) *The Prelude,* by William Wordsworth
6) *The Idea of the Holy,* by Rudolf Otto

7) *The Consolation of Philosophy,* by Boethius

8) *Life of Samuel Johnson,* by James Boswell

9) *Descent into Hell,* by Charles Williams

10) *Theism and Humanism,* by Arthur James Balfour

The Christian Century, June 6, 1962

How right you are when you say "Christianity is a terrible thing for a lifelong atheist to have to face"! In people like us—adult converts in the 20th century—I take this feeling to be a good symptom. . . . Now about reading.

For a good ("popular") defence of our position against modern waffle, to fall back on, I know nothing better than G. K. Chesterton's *The Everlasting Man.* Harder reading, but very protective, is Edwyn Bevan's *Symbolism & Belief.* Charles Williams' *He Came Down from Heaven* doesn't suit everyone, but try it.

For meditative and devotional reading (a little bit at a time, more like sucking a lozenge than eating a slice of bread) I suggest the *Imitation of Christ* (astringent) and Traherne's *Centuries of Meditations* (joyous). Also my selection from MacDonald, *Geo. MacDonald: an Anthology.* I can't read Kierkegaard myself, but some people find him helpful.

For Christian morals I suggest my wife's (Joy Davidman) <u>Smoke on the Mountain,</u> Gore's *The Sermon on the Mount* and (perhaps) his *Philosophy of the Good Life.* And possibly (but with a grain of salt, for he is too puritanical) Wm. Law's *Serious Call to a Devout and Holy Life.* I know the v. title makes me shudder, but we have both got a lot of shuddering to get through before we're done!

You'll want a mouth-wash for the imagination. I'm told that Mauriac's novels (all excellently translated, if your French is rusty) are good, tho' very severe. Dorothy Sayers' *Man Born to be King* (those broadcast plays) certainly is. So, to me, but not to everyone, are Charles Williams's fantastic novels. *Pilgrim's Progress,* if you ignore some straw-splitting dialogues in Calvinist theology and concentrate on the story, is first class.

St. Augustine's *Confessions* will give you the record of an earlier adult convert, with many v. great devotional passages intermixed.

Do you read poetry? George Herbert at his best is extremely nutritious.

I don't mention the Bible because I take that for granted. A modern translation is for most purposes far more useful than the Authorised Version.

As regards my own books, you might (or might not) care for *Transposition, The Great Divorce,* or *The Four Loves.*

The Collected Letters of C. S. Lewis, Volume III

CELEBRATION

"The Great Dance does not wait to be perfect until the peoples of the Low Worlds are gathered into it. We speak not of when it will begin. It has begun from before always. There was no time when we did not rejoice before His face as now. The dance which we dance is at the centre and for the dance all things were made. Blessed be He!"

Another said, "Never did He make two things the same; never did He utter one word twice. After earths, not better earths but beasts; after beasts, not better beasts but spirits. After a falling, not recovery but a new creation. Out of the new creation, not a third but the mode of change itself is changed for ever. Blessed be He!"

And another said, "It is loaded with justice as a tree bows down with fruit. All is righteousness and there is no equality. Not as when stones lie side by side, but as when stones support and are supported in an arch, such is His order; rule and obedience, begetting and bearing, heat glancing down, life growing up. Blessed be He!"

One said, "They who add years to years in lumpish aggregation, or miles to miles and galaxies to galaxies, shall not come near His greatness. The day of the fields of Arbol will fade and the days of Deep Heaven itself are numbered. Not thus is He great. He dwells (all of Him dwells) within the seed of the smallest flower and is not cramped: Deep Heaven is inside Him who is inside the seed and does not distend Him. Blessed be He!"

"The edge of each nature borders on that whereof it contains no shadow or similitude. Of many points one line; of many lines one shape; of many shapes one solid body; of many senses and thoughts one person; of three persons, Himself. As is the circle to the sphere, so are the ancient worlds that needed no redemption to that world wherein He was born and died. As is a point to a line, so is that world to the far-off fruits of its redeeming. Blessed be He!"

"Yet the circle is not less round than the sphere, and the sphere is the home and fatherland of circles. Infinite multitudes of circles lie enclosed in every sphere, and if they spoke they would say, For us were spheres created. Let no mouth open to gainsay them. Blessed be He!"

"The peoples of the ancient worlds who never sinned, for whom He never came down, are the peoples for whose sake the Low Worlds were made. For though the healing what was wounded and the straightening what was bent is a new dimension of glory, yet the straight was not made that it might be bent nor the whole that it might be wounded. The ancient peoples are at the centre. Blessed be He!"

"All which is not itself the Great Dance was made in order that He might come down into it. In the Fallen World He prepared for Himself a body and was united with the Dust and made it glorious for ever. This is the end and final cause of all creating, and the sin whereby it came is called Fortunate and the world where this was enacted is the centre of worlds. Blessed be He!"

Perelandra

"Oh, children," said the Lion, "I feel my strength coming back to me. <u>Oh, children, catch me if you can!</u>" He stood for a second, his eyes very bright, his limbs quivering, lashing himself with his tail. Then he made a leap high over their heads and landed on the other side of the Table. Laughing, though she didn't know why, Lucy scrambled over it to reach him. Aslan leaped again. A mad chase began. Round and round the hill-top he led them, now hopelessly out of their reach, now letting them almost catch his tail, now diving between them, now tossing them in the air with his huge and beautifully velveted paws and catching them again, and now stopping unexpectedly so that all three of them rolled over together in a happy laughing heap of fur and arms and legs. It was such a romp as no one has ever had except in Narnia; and whether it was more like playing with a thunderstorm or playing with a kitten Lucy could never make up her mind. And the funny thing was that <u>when all three finally lay together panting in the sun the girls no longer felt in the least tired or hungry or thirsty.</u>

The Lion, the Witch and the Wardrobe

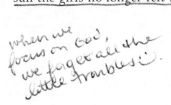

when we focus on God, we forget all the little troubles :).

CHARACTER

Surely what a man does when he is taken off his guard is the best evidence for what sort of a man he is? Surely what pops out before the man has time to put on a disguise is the truth? If there are rats in a cellar you are most likely to see them if you go in very suddenly. But the suddenness does not create the rats: it only prevents them from hiding. In the same way the suddenness of the provocation does not make me an ill-tempered man: it only shows me what an ill-tempered man I am.

Mere Christianity

Rats in the cellar

CHASTITY

Love of every sort is a guard against lust, even, by a divine paradox, sexual love is a guard against lust. No woman is more easily and painlessly abstained from, if need be, than the woman one loves.

The Collected Letters of C. S. Lewis, Volume III

We must now consider Christian morality as regards sex, what Christians call the virtue of chastity. The Christian rule of chastity must not be confused with the social rule of "modesty" (in one sense of that word); i.e., propriety, or decency. The social rule of propriety lays down how much of the human body should be displayed and what subjects can be referred to, and in what words, according to the customs of a given social circle. Thus, while the rule of chastity is the same for all Christians at all times, the rule of propriety changes. A girl in the Pacific islands wearing hardly any clothes and a Victorian lady completely covered in clothes might both be equally "modest," proper, or decent, according to the standards of their own societies: and both, for all we could tell by their dress, might be equally chaste (or equally unchaste). Some of the language which chaste women used in Shakespeare's time would have been used in the nineteenth century only by a woman completely abandoned. When people break the rule of propriety current in their own time and place, if they do so in order to excite lust in themselves or others, then they are offending against chastity. But if they break it through ignorance or carelessness they are guilty only of bad manners. When, as often happens, they break it defiantly in order to shock or embarrass others, they are not necessarily being unchaste, but they are being uncharitable: for it is uncharitable to take pleasure in making other people uncomfortable. I do not think that a very strict or fussy standard of propriety is any proof of chastity or any help to it, and I therefore regard the great relaxation and simplifying of the rule which has taken place in my own lifetime as a good thing. At its present stage, however, it has this inconvenience, that people of different ages and different types do not all acknowledge the same standard, and we hardly know where we are. While this confusion lasts I think that old, or old-fashioned, people should be very careful not to assume that young or "emancipated" people are corrupt whenever they are (by the old standard) improper; and, in return, that young people should not call their elders prudes or puritans because they do not easily adopt the new standard. A real desire to believe all the good you can of others and to make others as comfortable as you can will solve most of the problems.

Chastity is the most unpopular of the Christian virtues. There is no getting away from it: the old Christian rule is, "Either marriage, with complete faithfulness to your partner, or else total abstinence." Now this is so difficult and so contrary to our instincts, that obviously either Christianity is wrong or our sexual instinct, as it now is, has gone wrong. One or the other. Of course, being a Christian, I think it is the instinct which has gone wrong.

Mere Christianity

[The demon Screwtape writes:] Keep [the patient] wondering what pride or lack of faith has delivered him into your hands when a simple enquiry into what he has been eating or drinking for the last twenty-four hours would show him whence your ammunition comes and thus enable him by a very little abstinence to imperil your lines of communication. If he must think of the medical side of chastity, feed him the grand lie which we have made the English humans believe, that physical exercise in excess and consequent fatigue are specially favourable to this virtue. How they can believe this, in face of the notorious lustfulness of sailors and soldiers, may well be asked. But we used the schoolmasters to put the story about—men who were really interested in chastity as an excuse for games and therefore recommended games as an aid to chastity.

I note with great displeasure that the Enemy [God] has, for the time being, put a forcible end to your direct attacks on the patient's chastity. You ought to have known that He always does in the end, and you ought to have stopped before you reached that stage. For as things are, your man has now discovered the dangerous truth that these attacks don't last forever; consequently you cannot use again what is, after all, our best weapon—the belief of ignorant humans, that there is no hope of getting rid of us except by yielding. I suppose you've tried persuading him that chastity is unhealthy?

The Screwtape Letters

CHRISTIANITY

A perfect practice of Christianity would, of course, consist in a perfect imitation of the life of Christ—I mean, in so far as it was applicable in one's own particular circumstances. Not in an idiotic sense—it doesn't mean that every Christian should grow a beard, or be a bachelor, or become a travelling preacher. It means that every single act and feeling, every experience, whether pleasant or unpleasant, must be referred to God.

God in the Dock

I believe in Christianity as I believe that the sun has risen; not only because I see it, but because by it I see everything else.

The Weight of Glory

"That they all may be one" is a petition which in my prayers I never omit. While the wished-for unity of doctrine and order is missing, all the more eagerly let us try to keep the bond of charity: which alas, your people in Spain and ours in Northern Ireland do not.

The Collected Letters of C. S. Lewis, Volume III

We are all rightly distressed, and ashamed also, at the divisions of Christendom. But those who have always lived within the Christian fold may be too easily dispirited by them. They are bad, but such people do not know what it looks like from without.

Seen from there, what is left intact, despite all the divisions, still appears (as it truly is) an immensely formidable unity.

God in the Dock

I believe that, in the present divided state of Christendom, those who are at the heart of each division are all closer to one another than those who are at the fringes. I wd. even carry this beyond the borders of Christianity: how much more one has in common with a real Jew or Muslim than with a wretched liberalising, occidentalised specimen of the same categories.

Let us by all means pray for one another: it is perhaps the only form of "work for re-union" which never does anything but good.

The Collected Letters of C. S. Lewis, Volume III

I sometimes have a bright dream of re-union engulfing us unawares, like a great wave from behind our backs, perhaps at the very moment when our official representatives are still pronouncing it impossible. Discussions usually separate us; actions sometimes unite us.

Letters to Malcolm: Chiefly on Prayer

It is a wonderful thing and a strengthening of faith that two souls differing from each other in place, nationality, language, obedience and age should have been thus led into a delightful friendship; so far does the order of spiritual beings transcend the material order.

It makes easier that necessary doctrine that we are most closely joined together alike with the sinner Adam and with the Just One,

Jesus, even though as to body, time and place we have lived so differently from both. This unity of the whole human race exists: would that there existed that nobler union of which you write. No day do I let pass without my praying for that longed-for consummation.

The Collected Letters of C. S. Lewis, Volume III

To the very last, when two people differ in doctrine, logic proclaims that though both might be in error, it is impossible for both to be right. And error always to some extent disables.

When therefore we find a certain heavenly unity existing between really devout persons of differing creeds, a mutual understanding and even a power of mutual edification which each may lack towards a lukewarm member of his own denomination, we must ascribe this to the work of Christ, who, in the erroneous one, sterilizes his errors and inhibits the evil consequences they would naturally have ("If ye drink any deadly thing it shall not hurt you" [Mark 16:18]) and opens the eyes of the other party to all the truths mingled in his friend's errors, which are, of course, likely to be truths he particularly needs.

C. S. Lewis: Essay Collection and Other Short Pieces

If ever the book which I am not going to write is written, it must be the full confession by Christendom of Christendom's specific contribution to the sum of human cruelty and treachery. Large areas of "the World" will not hear us till we have publicly disowned much of our past. Why should they? We have shouted the name of Christ and enacted the service of Moloch.

The Four Loves

And let me make it quite clear that when Christians say the Christ-life is in them, they do not mean simply something mental or moral. When they speak of being "in Christ" or of Christ being "in them," this is not simply a way of saying that they are thinking about Christ or copying Him. They mean that Christ is actually operating through them; that the whole mass of Christians are the physical organism through which Christ acts—that we are His fingers and muscles, the cells of His body.

There was a time when every man was part of his mother, and (earlier still) part of his father as well: and when they were part of his grandparents. If you could see humanity spread out in time, as God sees it, it would not look like a lot of separate things dotted about. It would look like one single growing thing—rather like a very complicated tree. Every individual would appear connected with every other. And not only that. Individuals are not really separate from God any more than from one another. Every man, woman, and child all over the world is feeling and breathing at this moment only because God, so to speak, is "keeping him going."

Consequently, when Christ becomes man it is not really as if you could become one particular tin soldier. It is as if something which is always affecting the whole human mass begins, at one point, to affect that whole human mass in a new way. From that point the effect spreads through all mankind. It makes a difference to people who lived before Christ as well as to people who lived after Him. It makes a difference to people who have never heard of Him. It is like dropping into a glass of water one drop of something which gives a new taste or a new colour to the whole lot. But, of course, none of these illustrations really works perfectly. In the long run God is no one but Himself and what He does is like nothing else. You could hardly expect it to be.

Mere Christianity

The Christian life defends the single personality from the collective, not by isolating him but by giving him the status of an organ in the mystical Body. As the book of Revelation says, he is made "a pillar in the temple of God"; and it adds, "he shall go no more out." That introduces a new side of our subject. That structural position in the Church which the humblest Christian occupies is eternal and even cosmic. The Church will outlive the universe; in it the individual person will outlive the universe. Everything that is joined to the immortal head will share His immortality. We hear little of this from the Christian pulpit today. . . . If we do not believe it, let us be honest and relegate the Christian faith to museums. If we do, let us give up the pretence that it makes no difference. For this is the real answer to every excessive claim made by the collective. It is mortal; we shall live forever. There will come a time when every culture, every institution, every nation, the human race, all biological life, is extinct, and every one of us is still alive. Immortality is promised to us, not to these generalities. It was not for societies or states that Christ died, but for men. In that sense Christianity must seem to secular collectivists to involve an almost frantic assertion of individuality. But then it is not the individual as such who will share Christ's victory over death. We shall share the victory by being in the Victor. A rejection, or in Scripture's strong language, a crucifixion of the natural self is the passport to everlasting life. Nothing that has not died will be resurrected. That is just how Christianity cuts across the antithesis between individualism and collectivism. There lies the maddening ambiguity of our faith as it must appear to outsiders. It sets its face relentlessly against our natural individualism; on the other hand, it gives back to those who abandon individualism an eternal possession of their own personal being, even of their bodies. As mere biological entities, each with its separate will to live and to expand, we are apparently of no account; we are cross-fodder. But as organs in the Body of Christ, as stones and pillars in the temple, we are assured of our eternal self-identity and shall live to remember the galaxies as an old tale.

The Weight of Glory

There are three things that spread the Christ life to us: baptism, belief, and that mysterious action which different Christians call by different names—Holy Communion, the Mass, the Lord's Supper.

If you have once accepted Christianity, then some of its main doctrines shall be deliberately held before your mind for some time every day. That is why daily prayers and religious reading and churchgoing are necessary parts of the Christian life. We have to be continually reminded of what we believe. Neither this belief nor any other will automatically remain alive in the mind. It must be fed.

Mere Christianity

If I have read the New Testament aright, it leaves no room for "creativeness" even in a modified or metaphorical sense. Our whole destiny seems to lie in the opposite direction, in being as little as possible ourselves, in acquiring a fragrance that is not our own but borrowed, in becoming clean mirrors filled with the image of a face that is not ours. I am not here supporting the doctrine of total depravity, and I do not say that the New Testament supports it; I am saying only that the highest good of a creature must be creaturely—that is, derivative or reflective—good. In other words, as St. Augustine makes plain (De Civ. Dei xii, cap. I), pride does not only go before a fall but is a fall—a fall of the creature's attention from what is better, God, to what is worse, itself.

Christian Reflections

CHURCH

Enemy-occupied territory—that is what this world is. Christianity is the story of how the rightful king has landed, you might say landed in disguise, and is calling us all to take part in a great campaign of sabotage. When you go to church you are really listening in to the secret wireless from our friends: that is why the enemy is so anxious to prevent us from going.

When a young man who has been going to church in a routine way honestly realises that he does not believe in Christianity and stops going—provided he does it for honesty's sake and not just to annoy his parents—the spirit of Christ is probably nearer to him then than it ever was before.

Mere Christianity

When I first became a Christian, about fourteen years ago, I thought that I could do it on my own, by retiring to my rooms and reading theology, and I wouldn't go to the churches and Gospel Halls; and then later I found that it was the only way of flying your flag; and, of course, I found that this meant being a target. It is extraordinary how inconvenient to your family it becomes for you to get up early to go to Church. It doesn't matter so much if you get up early for anything else, but if you get up early to go to Church it's very selfish of you and you upset the house. If there is anything in the teaching of the New Testament which is in the nature of a command, it is that you are obliged to take the Sacrament, and you can't do it without going to Church.

God in the Dock

The New Testament does not envisage solitary religion: some kind of regular assembly for worship and instruction is everywhere taken for granted in the Epistles. So we must be regular practising members of the Church.

The Collected Letters of C. S. Lewis, Volume III

No Christian and, indeed, no historian could accept the epigram which defines religion as "what a man does with his solitude." It was one of the Wesleys, I think, who said that the New Testament knows nothing of solitary religion. We are forbidden to neglect the assembling of ourselves together. Christianity is already institutional in the earliest of its documents. The Church is the Bride of Christ. We are members of one another.

The Weight of Glory

God does not only "demand" praise as the supremely beautiful and all-satisfying Object. He does apparently command it as lawgiver. The Jews were told to sacrifice. We are under an obligation to go to church.

Reflections on the Psalms

The advantage of a fixed form of service is that we know what is coming. Ex tempore public prayer has this difficulty: we don't know whether we can mentally join in it until we've heard it—it might be phoney or heretical. We are therefore called upon to carry on a critical and a devotional activity at the same moment: two things hardly compatible. In a fixed form we ought to have "gone through the motions" before in our private prayers: the rigid form really sets our devotions free.

I also find the more rigid it is, the easier it is to keep one's thoughts from straying. Also it prevents any service getting too completely eaten up by whatever happens to be the pre-occupation of the moment (a war, an election, or what not). The permanent shape of Christianity shows through. I don't see how the ex tempore method can help becoming provincial & I think it has a great tendency to direct attention to the minister rather than to God.

The Collected Letters of C. S. Lewis, Volume III

COMFORT

God is the only comfort. He is also the supreme terror: the thing we most need and the thing we most want to hide from. He is our only possible ally, and we have made ourselves His enemies. Some people talk as if meeting the gaze of absolute goodness would be fun. They need to think again. They are still only playing with religion. Goodness is either the great safety or the great danger—according to the way you react to it. And we have reacted the wrong way. . . . Of course, I quite agree that the Christian religion is, in the long run, a thing of unspeakable comfort. But it does not begin in comfort; it begins in the dismay I have been describing, and it is no use at all trying to go on to that comfort without first going through that dismay. In religion, as in war and everything else, comfort is the one thing you cannot get by looking for it. If you look for truth, you may find comfort in the end: if you look for comfort you will not get either comfort or truth—only soft soap and wishful thinking to begin with and, in the end, despair.

Mere Christianity

Talk to me about the truth of religion and I'll listen gladly. Talk to me about the duty of religion and I'll listen submissively. But don't come talking to me about the consolations of religion or I shall suspect that you don't understand.

A Grief Observed

COMMUNION

The only rite which we know to have been instituted by Our Lord Himself is the Holy Communion ("Do this in remembrance of me"—"If you do not eat the flesh of the Son of Man and drink His blood, ye have no life in you"). This is an order and must be obeyed.

The Collected Letters of C. S. Lewis, Volume III

As for . . . the serious Christian godfather, I feel very unfit for the work—just as you, I dare say, may feel very unfit for being confirmed and for receiving the Holy Communion. But then an angel would not be really fit and we must all do the best we can. So I suppose I must try to give you advice. And the bit of advice that comes into my head is this; don't expect (I mean, don't count on and don't demand) that when you are confirmed, or when you make your first Communion, you will have all the feelings you would like to have. You may, of course: but also you may not. But don't worry if you don't get them. They aren't what matter. The things that are happening to you are quite real things whether you feel as you wd. wish or not, just as a meal will do a hungry person good even if he has a cold in the head which will rather spoil the taste. Our Lord will give us right feelings if He wishes—and then we must say Thank you. If He doesn't, then we must say to ourselves (and Him) that He knows us best. This, by the way, is one of the very few subjects on which I feel I do know something. For years after I had become a regular communicant I can't tell you how dull my feelings were and how my attention wandered at the most important moments. It is only in the last year or two that things have begun to come right—which just shows how important it is to keep on doing what you are told.

C. S. Lewis: Letters to Children

Next to the Blessed Sacrament itself, your neighbour is the holiest object presented to your senses. If he is your Christian neighbour he is holy in almost the same way, for in him also Christ *vere latitat* ["is truly hidden"]—the glorifier and the glorified, Glory Himself, is truly hidden.

The Weight of Glory

You ask me why I've never written anything about the Holy Communion. For the very simple reason that I am not good enough at Theology. I have nothing to offer. Hiding any light I think I've got under a bushel is not my besetting sin! I am much more prone to prattle unseasonably. But there is a point at which even I would gladly keep silent. The trouble is that people draw conclusions even from silence. Someone said in print the other day that I seemed to "admit rather than welcome" the sacraments.

I wouldn't like you and Betty to think the same. But as soon as I try to tell you anything more, I see another reason for silence. It is almost impossible to state the negative effect which certain doctrines have on me—my failure to be nourished by them—without seeming to mount an attack against them. But the very last thing I want to do is to unsettle in the mind of any Christian, whatever his denomination, the concepts—for him traditional—by which he finds it profitable to represent to himself what is happening when he receives the bread and wine. I could wish that no definitions had ever been felt to be necessary; and, still more, that none had been allowed to make divisions between churches. . . .

I find no difficulty in believing that the veil between the worlds, nowhere else (for me) so opaque to the intellect, is nowhere else so thin and permeable to divine operation. Here a hand from the hidden country touches not only my soul but my body. Here the prig, the don, the modern in me have no privilege over the savage or the child. Here is big medicine and strong magic. . . .

I hope I do not offend God by making my Communions in the frame of mind I have been describing. The command, after all, was Take, eat: not Take, understand. Particularly, I hope I need not be tormented by the question "What is this?"—this wafer, this sip of wine. That has a dreadful effect on me. It invites me to take "this" out of its holy context and regard it as an object among objects, indeed as part of nature. It is like taking a red coal out of the fire to examine it: it becomes a dead coal. To me, I mean. All this is autobiography, not theology.

Letters to Malcolm: Chiefly on Prayer

By the bye, what are your views, now, on the question of sacraments? To me that is the most puzzling side of the whole thing. I need hardly say I feel none of the materialistic difficulties: but I feel strongly just the opposite ones—i.e., I see (or think I see) so well a sense in which all wine is the blood of God—or all matter, even, the body of God, that I stumble at the apparently special sense in which this is claimed for the Host when consecrated. George Macdonald observes that the good man should aim at reaching the state of mind in which all meals are sacraments. Now that is the sort of thing I can understand: but I find no connection between it and the explicit "sacrament" *proprement dit* ["properly so called"]. The Presbyterian method of sitting at tables munching actual slices of bread is clearly absurd under ordinary conditions: but one can conceive a state of society in which a real meal might be shared by a congregation in such a way as to be a sacrament without ceasing to be also their actual dinner for that day. Possibly this was so in the very early Church.

The Collected Letters of C. S. Lewis, Volume II

CONFESSION

I think our official view of confession can be seen in the form for the Visitation of the Sick where it says "Then shall the sick person be moved (i.e., advised, prompted) to make a . . . Confession . . . if he feel his conscience troubled with any weighty matter." That is, where Rome makes Confession compulsory for all, we make it permissible for any: not "generally necessary" but profitable. We do not doubt that there can be forgiveness without it. But, as your own experience shows, many people do not feel forgiven, i.e., do not effectively "believe in the forgiveness of sins," without it. The quite enormous advantage of coming really to believe in forgiveness is well worth the horrors (I agree, they are horrors) of a first confession.

Also, there is the gain in self-knowledge: most of [us] have never really faced the facts about ourselves until we uttered them aloud in plain words, calling a spade a spade. I certainly feel I have profited enormously by the practice. At the same time I think we are quite right not to make it generally obligatory, which wd. force it on some who are not ready for it and might do harm.

The Collected Letters of C. S. Lewis, Volume III

CONSCIENCE

All men at times obey their vices: but it is when cruelty, envy, and lust of power appear as the commands of a great super-personal force that they can be exercised with self-approval. The first symptom is in language. When to "kill" becomes to "liquidate" the process has begun. The pseudo-scientific word disinfects the thing of blood and tears, or pity and shame, and mercy itself can be regarded as a sort of untidiness.

C. S. Lewis on Stories

Human beings, all over the earth, have this curious idea that they ought to behave in a certain way, and cannot really get rid of it.

Mere Christianity

How do we decide what is good or evil? The usual answer is that we decide by conscience. But probably no one thinks now of conscience as a separate faculty, like one of the senses. Indeed, it cannot be so thought of. For an autonomous faculty like a sense cannot be argued with; you cannot argue a man into seeing green if he sees blue. But the conscience can be altered by argument; and if you did not think so, you would not have asked me to come and argue with you about the morality of obeying the civil law when it tells us to serve in the wars. Conscience, then, means the whole man engaged in a particular subject matter.

But even in this sense conscience still has two meanings. It can mean (a) the pressure a man feels upon his will to do what he thinks is right; (b) his judgment as to what the content of right and wrong are. In sense (a) conscience is always to be followed. It is the sovereign of the universe, which "if it had power as it has right, would absolutely rule the world." It is not to be argued with, but obeyed, and even to question it is to incur guilt. But in sense (b) it is a very different matter. People may be mistaken about wrong and right; most people in some degree are mistaken. By what means are mistakes in this field to be corrected?

The Weight of Glory

CONSCIOUSNESS

And what am I? The façade is what I call consciousness. I am at least conscious of the colour of those walls. I am not, in the same way, or to the same degree, conscious of what I call my thoughts: for if I try to examine what happens when I am thinking, it stops happening. Yet even if I could examine my thinking, it would, I well know, turn out to be the thinnest possible film on the surface of a vast deep. The psychologists have taught us that. Their real error lies in underestimating the depth and the variety of its contents.

Letters to Malcolm: Chiefly on Prayer

CONTRITION

The Lenten season is devoted especially to what theologians call contrition, and so every day in Lent a prayer is said in which we ask God to give us "contrite hearts." Contrite, as you know, is a word translated from Latin, meaning crushed or pulverized. Now modern people complain that there is too much of that note in our Prayer Book. They do not wish their hearts to be pulverized, and they do not feel that they can sincerely say that they are "miserable offenders." I once knew a regular churchgoer who never repeated the words, "the burden of them (i.e., his sins) is intolerable," because he did not feel that they were intolerable. But he was not understanding the words. I think the Prayer Book is very seldom talking primarily about our feelings; that is (I think) the first mistake we're apt to make about these words "we are miserable offenders." I do not think whether we are feeling miserable or not matters. I think it is using the word miserable in the old sense—meaning an object of pity.

God in the Dock

CONVERSION

Every story of conversion is the story of a blessed defeat.

Smoke on the Mountain, by Joy Davidman

Take the case of a sour old maid, who is a Christian, but cantankerous. On the other hand, take some pleasant and popular fellow, but who has never been to Church. Who knows how much more cantankerous the old maid might be if she were not a Christian, and how much more likeable the nice fellow might be if he were a Christian? You can't judge Christianity simply by comparing the product in those two people; you would need to know what kind of raw material Christ was working on in both cases.

God in the Dock

Before I became a Christian I do not think I fully realized that one's life, after conversion, would inevitably consist in doing most of the same things one had been doing before, one hopes, in a new spirit, but still the same things.

The Weight of Glory

The world does not consist of 100 per cent Christians and 100 per cent non-Christians. There are people (a great many of them) who are slowly ceasing to be Christians but who still call themselves by that name: some of them are clergymen. There are other people who are slowly becoming Christian though they do not yet call themselves so. There are people who do not accept the full

Christian doctrine about Christ but who are so strongly attracted by Him that they are His in a much deeper sense than they themselves understand. There are people in other religions who are being led by God's secret influence to concentrate on those parts of their religion which are in agreement with Christianity, and who thus belong to Christ without knowing it.

Mere Christianity

It is right and inevitable that we shd. be much concerned about the salvation of those we love. But we must be careful not to expect or demand that their salvation shd. conform to some ready-made pattern of our own. Some Protestant sects have gone very wrong about this. They have a whole programme of conversion etc., marked out, the same for everyone, and will not believe that anyone can be saved who doesn't go through it "just so." But (see the last chapter of my *Problem of Pain*) God has His own way with each soul. There is no evidence that St. John underwent the same kind of "conversion" as St. Paul. It's not essential to believe in the Devil; and I'm sure a man can get to Heaven without being accurate about Methuselah's age. Also, as Macdonald says "the time for saying comes seldom, the time for being is always here." What we practise, not (save at rare intervals) what we preach, is usually our great contribution to the conversion of others.

The Collected Letters of C. S. Lewis, Volume III

"I looked up and saw the very last thing I expected: a huge lion coming slowly towards me. And one queer thing was that there was no moon last night, but there was moonlight where the lion was. So it came nearer and nearer. I was terribly afraid of it. You may think that being a dragon, I could have knocked any lion out easily enough. But it wasn't that kind of fear. I wasn't afraid of it eating me, I was just afraid of it—if you can understand. Well, it came closer up to me and looked straight into my eyes. And I shut my eyes tight. But that wasn't any good because it told me to follow it."

"You mean it spoke?"

"I don't know. Now that you mention it, I don't think it did. But it told me all the same. And I knew I'd have to do what it told me, so I got up and followed it. And it led me a long way into the mountains. And there was always this moonlight over and round the lion wherever we went. So at last we came to the top of a mountain I'd never seen before and on the top of this mountain there was a garden—trees and fruit and everything. In the middle of it there was a well.

"I knew it was a well because you could see the water bubbling up from the bottom of it: but it was a lot bigger than most wells—like a very big, round bath with marble steps going down into it. The water was as clear as anything and I thought if I could get in there and bathe it would ease the pain in my leg. But the lion told me I must undress first. Mind you, I don't know if he said any words out loud or not.

"I was just going to say that I couldn't undress because I hadn't any clothes on when I suddenly thought that dragons are snaky sort of things and snakes can cast their skins. Oh, of course, thought I, that's what the lion means. So I started scratching myself and my scales began coming off all over the place. And then I scratched a little deeper and, instead of just scales coming off here and there, my whole skin started peeling off beautifully, like it does after an illness, or as if I was a banana. In a minute or two I just stepped out of it. I could see it lying there beside me, looking rather nasty. It was a most lovely feeling. So I started to go down into the well for my bathe.

"But just as I was going to put my foot into the water I looked down and saw that it was all hard and rough and wrinkled and scaly just as it had been before. Oh, that's all right, said I, it only means I had another smaller suit on underneath the first one, and I'll have to get out of it too. So I scratched and tore again and this under skin peeled off beautifully and out I stepped and left it lying beside the other one and went down to the well for my bathe.

"Well, exactly the same thing happened again. And I thought to myself, oh dear, how ever many skins have I got to take off? For I was longing to bathe my leg. So I scratched away for the third time and got off a third skin, just like the two others, and stepped out of it. But as soon as I looked at myself in the water I knew it had been no good.

"Then the lion said—but I don't know if it spoke—You will have to let me undress you. I was afraid of his claws, I can tell you, but I was pretty nearly desperate now. So I just lay flat down on my back to let him do it.

"The very first tear he made was so deep that I thought it had gone right into my heart. And when he began pulling the skin off, it hurt worse than anything I've ever felt. The only thing that made me able to bear it was just the pleasure of feeling the stuff peel off. You know—if you've ever picked the scab of a sore place. It hurts like billy-oh but it is such fun to see it coming away."

"I know exactly what you mean," said Edmund.

"Well, he peeled the beastly stuff right off—just as I thought I'd done it myself the other three times, only they hadn't hurt—and there it was lying on the grass: only ever so much thicker, and darker, and more knobbly looking than the others had been. And there was I as smooth and soft as a peeled switch and smaller than I had been. Then he caught hold of me—I didn't like that much for I was very tender underneath now that I'd no skin on—and threw me into the water. It smarted like anything but only for a moment. After that it became perfectly delicious and as soon as I started swimming and splashing I found that all the pain had gone from my arm. And then I saw why. I'd turned into a boy again. You'd think me simply phoney if I told you how I felt about my own arms. I know they've no muscle and are pretty mouldy compared with Caspian's, but I was so glad to see them.

"After a bit the lion took me out and dressed me—"

"Dressed you. With his paws?"

"Well, I don't exactly remember that bit. But he did somehow or other: in new clothes—the same I've got on now, as a matter of fact. And then suddenly I was back here. Which is what makes me think it must have been a dream."

"No. It wasn't a dream," said Edmund.

"Why not?"

"Well, there are the clothes, for one thing. And you have been—well, un-dragoned, for another."

"What do you think it was, then?" asked Eustace.

"I think you've seen Aslan," said Edmund.

The Voyage of the DAWN TREADER

But it is, I think, a gross exaggeration to picture the saving of a soul as being, normally, at all like the development from seed to flower. The very words repentance, regeneration, the New Man suggest something very different.

The Weight of Glory

Imagine yourself as a living house. God comes in to rebuild that house. At first, perhaps, you can understand what He is doing. He is getting the drains right and stopping the leaks in the roof and so on: you knew that those jobs needed doing and so you are not surprised. But presently He starts knocking the house about in a way that hurts abominably and does not seem to make sense. What on earth is He up to? The explanation is that He is building quite a different house from the one you thought of—throwing out a new wing here, putting on an extra floor there, running up towers, making courtyards. You thought you were going to be made into a decent little cottage: but He is building a palace. He intends to come and live in it Himself.

Already the new men are dotted here and there all over the earth. Some, as I have admitted, are still hardly recognisable: but others can be recognised. Every now and then one meets them. Their very voices and faces are different from ours: stronger, quieter, happier, more radiant. They begin where most of us leave off. They are, I say, recognisable; but you must know what to look for.

52

They will not be very like the idea of "religious people" which you have formed from your general reading. They do not draw attention to themselves. You tend to think that you are being kind to them when they are really being kind to you. They love you more than other men do, but they need you less. (We must get over wanting to be needed: in some goodish people, specially women, that is the hardest of all temptations to resist.) They will usually seem to have a lot of time: you will wonder where it comes from. When you have recognised one of them, you will recognise the next one much more easily. And I strongly suspect (but how should I know?) that they recognise one another immediately and infallibly, across every barrier of colour, sex, class, age, and even of creeds. In that way, to become holy is rather like joining a secret society. To put it at the very lowest, it must be great fun.

Mere Christianity

Mr. Wirt: In your book *Surprised by Joy* you remark that you were brought into the Faith kicking and struggling and resentful, with eyes darting in every direction looking for an escape. You suggest that you were compelled, as it were, to become a Christian. Do you feel that you made a decision at the time of your conversion?

Lewis: I would not put it that way. What I wrote in *Surprised by Joy* was that "before God closed in on me, I was in fact offered what now appears a moment of wholly free choice." But I feel my decision was not so important. I was the object rather than the subject in this affair. I was decided upon. I was glad afterwards at the way it came out, but at the moment what I heard was God saying, "Put down your gun and we'll talk."

Mr. Wirt: That sounds to me as if you came to a very definite point of decision.

Lewis: Well, I would say that the most deeply compelled action is also the freest action. By that I mean, no part of you is outside the action. It is a paradox. I expressed it in *Surprised by Joy* by saying that I chose, yet it really did not seem possible to do the opposite.

God in the Dock

CREATION

No philosophical theory which I have yet come across is a radical improvement on the words of Genesis, that "In the beginning God made Heaven and Earth."

Miracles

Creation seems to be delegation through and through. He will do nothing simply of Himself which can be done by creatures. I suppose this is because He is a giver. And He has nothing to give but Himself. And to give Himself is to do His deeds—in a sense, and on varying levels to be Himself—through the things He has made.

Letters to Malcolm: Chiefly on Prayer

All our language about such things, that of the theologian as well as that of the child, is crude. The real point is that the myths, even in their own terms, do not reach the idea of Creation in our sense at all. Things "come up out of" something or "are formed in" something. If the stories could, for the moment, be supposed true, they would still be stories about very early events in a process of development, a world-history, which was already going on. When the curtain rises in these myths there are always some "properties" already on the stage and some sort of drama is proceeding. You may say they answer the question "How did the play begin?" But that is an ambiguous question. Asked by the man who arrived ten minutes late it would be properly answered, say, with the words, "Oh, first three witches came in, and then there was a scene between an old king and a wounded soldier." That is the sort of question the myths are in fact answering. But the very different question: "How does a play originate? Does it write itself? Do the actors make it up as they go along? Or is there someone—not on the stage, not like the people on the stage—someone we don't see who invented it all and caused it to be?" This is rarely asked or answered.

We do of course find in Plato a clear Theology of Creation in the Judaic and Christian sense; the whole universe—the very conditions of time and space under which it exists—are produced by the will of a perfect, timeless, unconditioned God who is above and outside all that He makes. But this is an amazing leap (though not made without the help of Him who is the Father of lights) by an overwhelming theological genius; it is not ordinary Pagan religion.

Now we all understand of course the importance of this peculiarity in Judaic thought from a strictly and obviously religious point of view. But its total consequences, the ways in which it changes a man's whole mind and imagination, might escape us.

To say that God created Nature, while it brings God and Nature into relation, also separates them. What makes and what is made must be two, not one. Thus the doctrine of Creation in one sense empties Nature of divinity. How very hard this was to do and, still more, to keep on doing, we do not now easily realise. A passage from Job (not without its own wild poetry in it) may help us: "If I beheld the sun when it shined, or the moon walking in brightness; and my heart hath been secretly enticed, or my mouth kissed my hand; this also would be an iniquity" (31, 26–28). There is here no question of turning, in a time of desperate need, to devilish gods. The speaker is obviously referring to an utterly spontaneous impulse, a thing you might find yourself acting upon almost unawares. To pay some reverence to the sun or moon is apparently so natural; so apparently innocent. Perhaps in certain times and places it was really innocent. I would gladly believe that the gesture of homage offered to the moon was sometimes accepted by her Maker; in those times of ignorance which God "winked at" (Acts 17, 30). The author of Job, however, was not in that ignorance. If he had kissed his hand to the Moon it would have been iniquity. The impulse was a temptation; one which no European has felt for the last thousand years.

But in another sense the same doctrine which empties Nature of her divinity also makes her an index, a symbol, a manifestation, of the Divine. I must recall two passages quoted in an earlier chapter. One is that from Psalm 19 where the searching and cleansing sun becomes an image of the searching and cleansing Law. The other is from 36: "Thy mercy, O Lord, reacheth unto the heavens, and thy faithfulness unto the clouds. Thy righteousness standeth like the strong mountains, thy judgements are like the great deep" (5, 6). It is surely just because the natural objects are no longer taken to be themselves Divine that they can now be magnificent symbols of Divinity. There is little point in comparing a Sun-god with the Sun or Neptune with the great deep; there is much in comparing the Law with the Sun or saying that God's judgements are an abyss and a mystery like the sea.

Reflections on the Psalms

The Lion, whose eyes never blinked, stared at the animals as hard as if he was going to burn them up with his mere stare. And gradually a change came over them. The smaller ones—the rabbits, moles and such-like—grew a good deal larger. The very big ones—you noticed it most with the elephants—grew a little smaller. Many animals sat up on their hind legs. Most put their heads on one side as if they were trying very hard to understand. The Lion opened his mouth, but no sound came from it; he was breathing out, a long, warm breath; it seemed to sway all the beasts as the wind sways a line of trees. Far overhead from beyond the veil of blue sky which hid them the stars sang again: a pure, cold, difficult music. Then there came a swift flash like fire (but it burnt nobody) either from the sky or from the Lion itself, and every drop of blood tingled in the children's bodies, and the deepest, wildest voice they had ever heard was saying:

"Narnia, Narnia, Narnia, awake. Love. Think. Speak. Be walking trees. Be talking beasts. Be divine waters."

The Magician's Nephew

CRUCIFIXION

There is indeed one mental image which does not lure me away into trivial elaborations. I mean the Crucifixion itself; not seen in terms of all the pictures and crucifixes, but as we must suppose it to have been in its raw, historical reality. But even this is of less spiritual value than one might expect. Compunction, compassion, gratitude—all the fruitful emotions—are strangled. Sheer physical horror leaves no room for them. Nightmare. Even so, the image ought to be periodically faced. But no one could live with it. It did not become a frequent motive of Christian art until the generations which had seen real crucifixions were all dead. As for many hymns and sermons on the subject—endlessly harping on blood, as if that were all that mattered—they must be the work either of people so far above me that they can't reach me, or else of people with no imagination at all. (Some might be cut off from me by both these gulfs.)

Letters to Malcolm: Chiefly on Prayer

It costs God nothing, so far as we know, to create nice things: but to convert rebellious wills cost Him crucifixion.

Mere Christianity

In perfect cyclic movement, being, power and joy descended from God to man in the form of gift and returned from man to God in the form of obedient love and ecstatic adoration: and in this sense, though not in all, man was then truly the son of God, the prototype of Christ, perfectly enacting in joy and ease of all the faculties and all the senses that filial self-surrender which Our Lord enacted in the agonies of the crucifixion.

Now the fact that God can make complex good out of simple evil does not excuse—though by mercy it may save—those who do the simple evil. And this distinction is central. Offences must come, but woe to those by whom they come; sins do cause grace to abound, but we must not make that an excuse for continuing to sin. The crucifixion itself is the best, as well as the worst, of all historical events, but the role of Judas remains simply evil.

The Problem of Pain

CULTURE

[Every Christian] must ask himself how it is right, or even psychologically possible, for creatures who are every moment advancing either to heaven or to hell, to spend any fraction of the little time allowed them in this world on such comparative trivialities as literature or art, mathematics or biology. If human culture can stand up to that, it can stand up to anything.

The intellectual life is not the only road to God, nor the safest, but we find it to be a road, and it may be the appointed road for us. Of course it will be so only so long as we keep the impulse pure and disinterested. That is the great difficulty. As the author of the *Theologia Germanica* says, we may come to love knowledge—our knowing—more than the thing known: to delight not in the exercise of our talents but in the fact that they are ours, or even in the reputation they bring us. Every success in the scholar's life increases this danger. If it becomes irresistible, he must give up his scholarly work. The time for plucking out the right eye has arrived.

The Weight of Glory

DEATH

About death I go through different moods, but the times when I can desire it are never, I think, those when this world seems harshest. On the contrary, it is just when there seems to be most of Heaven already here that I come nearest to longing for a *patria* [homeland].

The Collected Letters of C. S. Lewis, Volume III

[The doctrine of Death] is an "eternal gospel" revealed to men wherever men have sought, or endured, the truth: it is the very nerve of redemption, which anatomising wisdom at all times and in all places lays bare; the unescapable knowledge which the Light that lighteneth every man presses down upon the minds of all who seriously question what the universe is "about."

The Problem of Pain

On the one hand Death is the triumph of Satan, the punishment of the Fall, and the last enemy. Christ shed tears at the grave of Lazarus and sweated blood in Gethsemane: the Life of Lives that was in Him detested this penal obscenity not less than we do, but more. On the other hand, only he who loses his life will save it. We are baptised into the death of Christ, and it is the remedy for the Fall. Death is, in fact, what some modern people call "ambivalent." It is Satan's great weapon and also God's great weapon: it is holy and unholy; our supreme disgrace and our only hope; the thing Christ came to conquer and the means by which He conquered.

Satan produced human Death. But when God created Man He gave him such a constitution that, if the highest part of it rebelled against Himself, it would be bound to lose control over the lower parts: i.e., in the long run to suffer Death. This provision may be regarded equally as a punitive sentence ("In the day ye eat of that fruit ye shall die"), as a mercy, and as a safety device. It is punishment because Death—that Death of which Martha says to Christ, "But . . . Sir . . . it'll smell"—is horror and ignominy. ("I am not so much afraid of death as ashamed of it," said Sir Thomas Browne.) It is mercy because by willing and humble surrender to it Man undoes his act of rebellion and makes even this depraved and monstrous mode of Death an instance of that higher and mystical Death which is eternally good and a necessary ingredient in the highest life. "The readiness is all"—not, of course, the merely heroic readiness but that of humility and self-renunciation. Our enemy, so welcomed, becomes our servant: bodily Death, the monster, becomes blessed spiritual Death to self, if the spirit so wills—or rather if it allows the Spirit of the willingly dying God so to will in it. It is a safety device because, once Man has fallen, natural immortality would be the one utterly hopeless destiny for him. Aided to the surrender that he must make by no external necessity of Death, free (if you call it freedom) to rivet faster and faster about himself through unending centuries the chains of his own pride and lust and of the nightmare civilisations which these build up in ever-increasing power and complication, he would progress from being merely a fallen man to being a fiend, possibly beyond all modes of redemption. This danger was averted. The sentence that those who ate of the forbidden fruit would be driven away from the Tree of Life was implicit in the composite nature with which Man was created. But to convert this penal death into the means of eternal life—to add to its negative and preventive function a positive and saving function—it was further necessary that death should be accepted. Humanity must embrace death freely, submit to it with total humility, drink it to the dregs, and so convert it into that mystical death which is the secret of life. But only a Man who did not need to have been a Man at all unless He had chosen, only one who served in our sad regiment as a volunteer, yet also one who was perfectly a Man, could perform this perfect dying; and thus (which way you put it is unimportant) either defeat Death or redeem it. He tasted death on behalf of all others. He is the representative "Die-er" of the universe: and for that very reason the Resurrection and the Life. Or conversely, because He truly lives, He truly dies, for that is the very pattern of reality. Because the higher can descend into the lower He who from all eternity has been incessantly plunging Himself in the blessed death of self-surrender to the Father can also most fully descend into the horrible and (for us) involuntary death of the body. Because Vicariousness is the very idiom of the reality He has created, His death can become ours. The whole Miracle, far from denying what we already know of reality, writes the comment which makes that crabbed text plain: or rather, proves itself to be the text on which Nature was only the commentary. In science we have been reading only the notes to a poem; in Christianity we find the poem itself.

Miracles

it was not involuntary for Christ!

in order to really die, you have to have something to lose.

in this way god meant & intended to death all commanded. Nonetheless, one need not have lived a good life to die at god + worthy death.

I must never, like the Stoics, say that death does not matter. Nothing is less Christian than that. Death which made Life Himself shed tears at the grave of Lazarus, and shed tears of blood in Gethsemane. This is an appalling horror; a stinking indignity. (You remember Thomas Browne's splendid remark: "I am not so much afraid of death, as ashamed of it.") And yet, somehow or other, infinitely good. Christianity does not simply affirm or simply deny the horror of death; it tells me something quite new about it.

God in the Dock

"I wonder," said the woman, "if you were sent here to teach us death."

"You don't understand," he said. "It is not like that. It is horrible. It has a foul smell. Maleldil Himself wept when He saw it."

Perelandra

What a state we have got into when we can't say "I'll be happy when God calls me" without being afraid one will be thought "morbid." After all, St. Paul said just the same. If we really believe what we say we believe—if we really think that home is elsewhere and that this life is a "wandering to find home," why should we not look forward to the arrival? There are, aren't there, only three things we can do about death: to desire it, to fear it, or to ignore it. The third alternative, which is the one the modern world calls "healthy," is surely the most uneasy and precarious of all.

[Death] happens to all of us, and I have no patience with the high-minded people who make out that it "doesn't matter." It matters a great deal, and very solemnly. And for those who are left, the pain is not the whole thing. I feel v. strongly (and I am not alone in this) that some good comes from the dead to the living in the months or weeks after the death. I think I was much helped by my own father after his death: as if our Lord welcomed the newly dead with the gift of some power to bless those they have left behind; His birthday present. Certainly, they often seem just at that time to be very near us.

The Collected Letters of C. S. Lewis, Volume III

"But," said Eustace, looking at Aslan. "Hasn't he—er—died?"

"Yes," said the Lion in a very quiet voice, almost (Jill thought) as if he were laughing. "He has died. Most people have, you know. Even I have. There are very few who haven't."

"Oh," said Caspian. "I see what's bothering you. You think I'm a ghost, or some nonsense. But don't you see? I would be that if I appeared in Narnia now: because I don't belong there any more. But one can't be a ghost in one's own country."

The Silver Chair

100 per cent of us die, and the percentage cannot be increased.

The Weight of Glory

"Proud people breed sad sorrows for themselves."
— *Wuthering Heights*

DEMONS

There are two equal and opposite errors into which our race can fall about the devils. One is to disbelieve in their existence. The other is to believe, and to feel an excessive and unhealthy interest in them. They themselves are equally pleased by both errors and hail a materialist or a magician with the same delight. The sort of script which is used in this book can be very easily obtained by anyone who has once learned the knack; but ill-disposed or excitable people who might make a bad use of it shall not learn it from me.

The Screwtape Letters, Preface

According to the Christians this [Nature's imperfection] is all due to sin: the sin both of men and of powerful, non-human beings, supernatural but created. The unpopularity of this doctrine arises from the widespread Naturalism of our age—the belief that nothing but Nature exists and that if anything else did she is protected from it by a Maginot Line—and will disappear as this error is corrected. To be sure, the morbid inquisitiveness about such beings, which led our ancestors to a pseudo-science of Demonology, is to be sternly discouraged: our attitude should be that of the sensible citizen in wartime who believes that there are enemy spies in our midst but disbelieves nearly every particular spy story.

Miracles

No reference to the Devil or devils is included in any Christian Creeds, and it is quite possible to be a Christian without believing in them. I do believe such beings exist, but that is my own affair. Supposing there to be such beings, the degree to which humans were conscious of their presence would presumably vary very much. I mean, the more a man was in the Devil's power, the less he would be aware of it, on the principle that a man is still fairly sober as long as he knows he's drunk. It is the people who are fully awake and trying hard to be good who would be most aware of the Devil. It is when you start arming against Hitler that you first realise your country is full of Nazi agents. Of course, they don't want you to believe in the Devil. If devils exist, their first aim is to give you an anaesthetic—to put you off your guard. Only if that fails, do you become aware of them.

God in the Dock

I believe [in the existence of the devil] not in the sense that it is part of my creed, but in the sense that it is one of my opinions. My religion would not be in ruins if this opinion were shown to be false. Till that happens—and proofs of a negative are hard to come by—I shall retain it. It seems to me to explain a good many facts. It agrees with the plain sense of Scripture, the tradition of Christendom, and the beliefs of most men at most times. And it conflicts with nothing that any of the sciences has shown to be true.

The Screwtape Letters

DENOMINATIONS

The reader should be warned that I offer no help to anyone who is hesitating between two Christian "denominations.". . . Our divisions should never be discussed except in the presence of those who have already come to believe that there is one God and that Jesus Christ is His only Son. . . .

I hope no reader will suppose that "mere" Christianity is here put forward as an alternative to the creeds of the existing communions—as if a man could adopt it in preference to Congregationalism or Greek Orthodoxy or anything else. It is more like a hall out of which doors open into several rooms. If I can bring anyone into that hall I shall have done what I attempted. But it is in the rooms, not in the hall, that there are fires and chairs and meals. The hall is a place to wait in, a place from which to try the various doors, not a place to live in. For that purpose the worst of the rooms (whichever that may be) is, I think, preferable. It is true that some people may find they have to wait in the hall for a considerable time, while others feel certain almost at once which door they must knock at. I do not know why there is this difference, but I am sure God keeps no one waiting unless He sees that it is good for him to wait. When you do get into your room you will find that the long wait has done you some kind of good which you would not have had otherwise. But you must regard it as waiting, not a camping. You must keep on praying for light: and, of course, even in the hall, you must begin trying to obey the rules which are common to the whole house. And above all you must be asking which door is the true one; not which pleases you best by its paint and panelling. In plain language, the question should never be: "Do I like that kind of service?" but "Are these doctrines true? Is holiness here? Does my conscience move me towards this? Is my reluctance to knock at this door due to my pride, or my mere taste, or my personal dislike of this particular door-keeper?"

When you have reached your own room, be kind to those who have chosen different doors and to those who are still in the hall. If they are wrong they need your prayers all the more; and if they are your enemies, then you are under orders to pray for them. That is one of the rules common to the whole house.

Mere Christianity

DEPRAVITY

This chapter will have been misunderstood if anyone describes it as a reinstatement of the doctrine of Total Depravity. I disbelieve that doctrine, partly on the logical ground that if our depravity were total we should not know ourselves to be depraved, and partly because experience shows us much goodness in human nature.

The Problem of Pain

DEPRESSION

My own idea, for what it is worth, is that all sadness which is not either arising from the repentance of a concrete sin and hastening towards concrete amendment or restitution, or else arising from pity and hastening to active assistance, is simply bad; and I think that we all sin by needlessly disobeying the apostolic injunction to "rejoice" as by anything else. Humility, after the first shock, is a cheerful virtue; it is the high-minded unbeliever desperately trying in the teeth of repeated disillusions to retain his "faith in human nature" who is really sad.

The Problem of Pain

"Human nature, after all, never really changes much."

—K

DESIRE

We are half-hearted creatures, fooling about with drink and sex and ambition when infinite joy is offered us, like an ignorant child who wants to go on making mud pies in a slum because he cannot imagine what is meant by the offer of a holiday at the sea. We are far too easily pleased.

Though I do not believe (I wish I did) that my desire for Paradise proves that I shall enjoy it, I think it a pretty good indication that such a thing exists and that some men will. A man may love a woman and not win her; but it would be very odd if the phenomenon called "falling in love" occurred in a sexless world.

The Weight of Glory

DIVINITY OF CHRIST

When people object, as you do, that if Jesus was God as well as Man, then He had an unfair advantage which deprives Him for them of all value, it seems to me as if a man struggling in the water shd. refuse a rope thrown to him by another who had one foot on the bank, saying "Oh, but you have an unfair advantage"; it is because of that advantage that He can help.

works this way with people too. Good, mediocre, weak, strong, etc.

Your view about the divinity of Christ was an old bone of contention between us, wasn't it? But I thought when we last met you had come down on the same side as me. I don't think I can agree that the Churches are empty because they teach that Jesus is God. If so, the ones that teach the opposite, i.e., the Unitarians, would be full, wouldn't they? Are they? It seems to me that the ones which teach the fullest and most dogmatic theology are precisely the ones that retain their people and make converts, while the liberalising and modernising ones lose ground every day. Thus the R.C.'s are flourishing and growing, and in the C. of E. the "high" churches are fuller than the "low." Not of course that I would accept popularity as a test of truth: only since you introduced it, I must say that as far as it is evidence at all it points the other way. And in history too. Your doctrine, under its old name of Arianism, was given a chance: in fact a v. full run for its money for it officially dominated the Roman Empire at one time. But it didn't last.

I think the great difficulty is this: if He was not God, who or what was He? In Matt. 28.19 you already get the baptismal formula "In the name of the Father, the Son, & the Holy Ghost." Who is this "Son"? Is the Holy Ghost a man? If not, does a man "send" Him (see John 15.26)? In Col. 1.12 [1:17] Christ is "before all things and by Him all things consist." What sort of a man is this? I leave out the obvious place at the beginning of St. John's Gospel. Take something much less obvious. When He weeps over Jerusalem (Matt. 23) why does He suddenly say (v. 34) "I send unto you prophets and wise men"? Who cd. say this except either God or a lunatic? Who is this man who goes about forgiving sins? Or what about Mark 2.18–19? What man can announce that—simply because he is present—acts of penitence, such as fasting, are "off"? Who can give the school a half holiday except the Headmaster?

The doctrine of Christ's divinity seems to me not something stuck on which you can unstick but something that peeps out at every point so that you'd have to unravel the whole web to get rid of it. Of course you may reject some of these passages as unauthentic, but then I cd. do the same to yours if I cared to play that game! When it says God can't be tempted I take this to be an obvious truth. God, as God, can't, any more than He can die. He became man precisely to do and suffer what as God He cd. not do and suffer. And if you take away the Godhead of Christ, what is Xtianity all about? How can the death of one man have this effect for all men which is proclaimed throughout the New Testament?

The Collected Letters of C. S. Lewis, Volume II

"Xmas"— I wonder if Xns wd be happier w/ the "X" if it looked more obviously like a cross.

DOUBT

Just as the Christian has his moments when the clamour of this visible and audible world is so persistent and the whisper of the spiritual world so faint that faith and reason can hardly stick to their guns, so, as I well remember, the atheist too has his moments of shuddering misgiving, of an all but irresistible suspicion that old tales may after all be true, that something or someone from outside may at any moment break into his neat, explicable, mechanical universe. Believe in God and you will have to face hours when it seems obvious that this material world is the only reality: disbelieve in Him and you must face hours when this material world seems to shout at you that it is not all. No conviction, religious or irreligious, will, of itself, end once and for all this fifth-columnist in the soul. Only the practice of Faith resulting in the habit of Faith will gradually do that.

Christian Reflections

As far as you (and I) are concerned I have no doubt that the fear you mention is simply a temptation of the devil, an effort to keep us away from God by despair. It is often the devil working through some defect in our health, and in extreme cases it needs a medical as well as a spiritual cure. So don't listen to these fears and doubts any more than you would to any obviously impure or uncharitable thoughts. . . . Of course, like other evil temptations, they will not be silenced at once. You will think you have got rid of them and then they will come back again—and again. But, with all our temptations of all sorts, we must just endure this. Keep on, do your duty, say your prayers, make your communions, and take no notice of the tempter. He goes away in the end. Remember I John iii, 20 "If (= though) our heart condemn us, God is greater than our heart."

The Collected Letters of C. S. Lewis, Volume III

"Though our heart condemn us,
God is greater than our heart."
— I John iii, 20

DUTY

I now see that I spent most of my life in doing neither what I ought nor what I liked.

The Screwtape Letters

Of course you are quite right if you mean that giving up fun for no reason except that you think it's "good" to give it up is all nonsense. Don't the ordinary old rules about telling the truth and doing as you'd be done by tell one pretty well which kinds of fun one may have and which not? But provided the thing is in itself right, the more one likes it and the less one has to "try to be good," the better. A perfect man wd. never act from sense of duty; he'd always want the right thing more than the wrong one. Duty is only a substitute for love (of God and of other people)—like a crutch, which is a substitute for a leg. Most of us need the crutch at times: but of course it's idiotic to use the crutch when our own legs (our own loves, tastes, habits, etc.) can do the journey on their own!

The Collected Letters of C. S. Lewis, Volume III

on how to live and to love the good things in life. How to enjoy the right kind of fun.

EASTER

Tomorrow we shall celebrate the glorious Resurrection of Christ. I shall be remembering you in the Holy communion. Away with tears and fears and troubles! United in wedlock with the eternal Godhead Itself, our nature ascends into the Heaven of Heavens, *worthy of pity* so it would be impious to call ourselves "miserable." On the contrary, man is a creature whom angels—were they capable of envy—would envy. Let us lift up our hearts!

The Collected Letters of C. S. Lewis, Volume II

There is a stage in a child's life at which it cannot separate the religious from the merely festal character of Christmas or Easter. I have been told of a very small and very devout boy who was heard murmuring to himself on Easter morning a poem of his own composition which began "Chocolate eggs and Jesus risen." This seems to me, for his age, both admirable poetry and admirable piety. But of course the time will soon come when such a child can no longer effortlessly and spontaneously enjoy that unity. He will become able to distinguish the spiritual from the ritual and festal aspect of Easter; chocolate eggs will no longer be sacramental. And once he has distinguished he must put one or the other first. If he puts the spiritual first he can still taste something of Easter in the chocolate eggs; if he puts the eggs first they will soon be no more than any other sweetmeat. They have taken on an independent, and therefore a soon withering, life.

Reflections on the Psalms

want to read

In adoration, more than in any other kind of prayer, the public or communal act is of the utmost importance. One would lose incomparably more by being prevented from going to church on Easter than on Good Friday.

Letters to Malcolm: Chiefly on Prayer

EPITAPH FOR HELEN JOY DAVIDMAN

Here the whole world (stars, water, air,
And field, and forest, as they were
Reflected in a single mind)
Like cast off clothes was left behind
In ashes yet with hope that she,
Re-born from holy poverty,
In lenten lands, hereafter may
Resume them on her Easter Day.

The Collected Poems of C. S. Lewis

we hopefully all get one!

ECOLOGY

In order to understand fully what Man's power over Nature, and therefore the power of some men over other men, really means, we must picture the race extended in time from the date of its emergence to that of its extinction. Each generation exercises power over its successors: and each, in so far as it modifies the environment bequeathed to it and rebels against tradition, resists and limits the power of its predecessors.

The Abolition of Man

It wd. be less terrifying if one cd. really attribute the murder of beauty to any particular set of evil men: the trouble is that from man's first and wholly legitimate attempt to win safety and ease from Nature it seems, step by step, to lead on quite logically to universal suburbia.

The Collected Letters of C. S. Lewis, Volume II

Since the Humans came into the land, felling forests and defiling streams, the Dryads and Naiads have sunk into a deep sleep. Who knows if ever they will stir again?

Prince Caspian

⌐ interesting study:
Lewis + Environmentalism; Nature and
the Chronicles of Narnia

EDUCATION

The student is half afraid to meet one of the great philosophers face to face. He feels himself inadequate and thinks he will not understand him. But if he only knew, the great man, just because of his greatness, is much more intelligible than his modern commentator. The simplest student will be able to understand, if not all, yet a very great deal of what Plato said; but hardly anyone can understand some modern books on Platonism. It has always therefore been one of my main endeavours as a teacher to persuade the young that first-hand knowledge is not only more worth acquiring than second-hand knowledge, but is usually much easier and more delightful to acquire.

God in the Dock

Schoolmasters in our time are fighting hard in defence of education against vocational training; universities, on the other hand, are fighting against education on behalf of learning.

Let me explain. The purpose of education has been described by Milton as that of fitting a man "to perform justly, skilfully, and magnanimously all the offices both private and public, of peace and war." Provided we do not overstress "skilfully" Aristotle would substantially agree with this, but would add the conception that it should also be a preparation for leisure, which according to him is the end of all human activity. "We wage war in order to have peace; we work in order to have leisure." Neither of them would dispute that the purpose of education is to produce the

82

good man and the good citizen, though it must be remembered that we are not here using the word "good" in any narrowly ethical sense. The "good man" here means the man of good taste and good feeling, the interesting and interested man, and almost the happy man. With such an end in view education in most civilised communities has taken much the same path; it has taught civil behaviour by direct and indirect discipline, has awakened the logical faculty by mathematics or dialectic, and has endeavoured to produce right sentiments—which are to the passions what right habits are to the body—by steeping the pupil in the literature both sacred and profane on which the culture of the community is based. Vocational training, on the other hand, prepares the pupil not for leisure, but for work; it aims at making not a good man but a good banker, a good electrician, a good scavenger, or a good surgeon. You see at once that education is essentially for freemen and vocational training for slaves. That is how they were distributed in the old unequal societies; the poor man's son was apprenticed to a trade, the rich man's son went to Eton and Oxford and then made the grand tour. When societies become, in effort if not in achievement, egalitarian, we are presented with a difficulty. To give every one education and to give no one vocational training is impossible, for electricians and surgeons we must have and they must be trained. Our ideal must be to find time for both education and training: our danger is that equality may mean training for all and education for none—that every one will learn commercial French instead of Latin, book-keeping instead of geometry, and "knowledge of the world we live in" instead of great literature. It is against this danger that schoolmasters have to fight, for if education is beaten by training, civilisation dies. That is a thing very likely to happen. One of the most dangerous errors instilled into us by nineteenth-century progressive optimism is the idea that civilisation is automatically bound to increase and spread. The lesson of history is the opposite; civilisation is a rarity, attained with difficulty and easily lost. The normal state of humanity is barbarism, just as the normal surface of our planet is salt water. Land looms large in our imagination of the planet and civilisation in our history books, only because sea and savagery are, to us, less interesting. And if you press to know what I mean by civilisation, I reply "Humanity," by which I do not mean kindness so much as the realization of the human idea. Human life means to me the life of beings for whom the leisured activities of thought, art, literature, conversation are the end, and the preservation and propagation of life merely the means.

That is why education seems to me so important: it actualises that potentiality for leisure, if you like for amateurishness, which is man's prerogative. You have noticed, I hope, that man is the only amateur animal; all the others are professionals. They have no leisure and do not desire it. When the cow has finished eating she chews the cud; when she has finished chewing she sleeps; when she has finished sleeping she eats again. She is a machine for turning grass into calves and milk—in other words, for producing more cows. The lion cannot stop hunting, nor the beaver building dams, nor the bee making honey. When God made the beasts dumb He saved the world from infinite boredom, for if they could speak; they would all of them, all day, talk nothing but shop.

Rehabilitations and Other Essays

The task of the modern educator is not to cut down jungles but to irrigate deserts.

The Abolition of Man

None can give to another what he does not possess himself. No generation can bequeath to its successor what it has not got. You may frame the syllabus as you please. But when you have planned and reported ad nauseam, if we are skeptical we shall teach only skepticism to our pupils, if fools only folly, if saints sanctity, if heroes heroism.

God in the Dock

what have I learned?
:goodness, justice + mercy, piety,
fun, joy, love of the good,
philosophy, some wisdom,
respect, understanding of subjects
and of other people.

EFFORT

Now we cannot . . . discover our failure to keep God's law except by trying our very hardest (and then failing). Unless we really try, whatever we say there will always be at the back of our minds the idea that if we try harder next time we shall succeed in being completely good. Thus, in one sense, the road back to God is a road of moral effort, of trying harder and harder. But in another sense it is not trying that is ever going to bring us home. All this trying leads up to the vital moment at which you turn to God and say, "You must do this. I can't."

Mere Christianity

Many things—such as loving, going to sleep, or behaving unaffectedly—are done worst when we try hardest to do them.

Studies in Medieval and Renaissance Literature

hmmm.

EMBARRASSMENT

People blush at praise—not only praise of their bodies, but praise of anything that is theirs. Most people exhibit some kind of modesty or bashfulness, at least at the beginning, in receiving any direct statement of another human being's affection for them, even if that affection is quite unrelated to sex or to the body at all. To be *valued* is an experience which involves a curious kind of self-consciousness. The subject is suddenly compelled to remember that it is also an object, and, apparently, an object intently regarded: hence, in a well-ordered mind, feelings of unworthiness and anxiety, mingled with delight, spring up. There seems to be a spiritual, as well as a physical, nakedness, fearful of being found ugly, embarrassed even at being found lovely, reluctant (even when not *amorously* reluctant) to be *found* at all.

A Preface to Paradise Lost

EMOTION

Don't be worried about feeling flat, or about feeling at all. As to what to do, I suppose the normal next step, after self-examination, repentance and restitution, is to make your Communion; and then to continue as well as you can, praying as well as you can . . . and fulfilling your daily duties as well as you can. And remember always that religious emotion is only a servant. . . . Don't worry if your heart won't respond; do the best you can. You are certainly under the guidance of the Holy Ghost, or you wouldn't have come where you now are; and the love that matters is His for you—yours for Him may at present exist only in the form of obedience. He will see to the rest.

The Collected Letters of C. S. Lewis, Volume II

One used to be told as a child: "Think what you're saying." Apparently we need also to be told: "Think what you're thinking." The stakes have to be raised before we take the game quite seriously. I know this is the opposite of what is often said about the necessity of keeping all emotion out of our intellectual processes—"you can't think straight unless you are cool." But then neither can you think deep if you are. I suppose one must try every problem in both states. You remember that the ancient Persians debated everything twice: once when they were drunk and once when they were sober. *ha!*

Letters to Malcolm: Chiefly on Prayer

By the way, don't "weep inwardly" and get a sore throat. <u>If you must weep, weep: a good honest howl</u>! I suspect we—and especially, my sex—don't cry enough now-a-days. Aeneas and Hector and Beowulf, Roland and Lancelot blubbered like schoolgirls, so why shouldn't we?

The Collected Letters of C. S. Lewis, Volume III

ENCORE

He had always disliked the people who encored a favourite air in an opera—"That just spoils it" had been his comment. But this now appeared to him as a principle of far wider application and deeper moment. This itch to have things over again, as if life were a film that could be unrolled twice or even made to work backwards . . . was it possibly the root of all evil? No: of course the love of money was called that. But money itself—perhaps one valued it chiefly as a defence against chance, a security for being able to have things over again, a means of arresting the unrolling of the film.

Perelandra

I love this book !

EQUALITY

[handwritten: resentfulness for what is subtler than oneself? like more graceful?]

The demand for equality has two sources: one of them is among the noblest, the other is the basest, of human emotions. The noble source is the desire for fair play. But the other source is the hatred of superiority. At the present moment it would be very unrealistic to overlook the importance of the latter. <u>There is in all</u> *[handwritten: Arthur]* <u>men a tendency</u> (only corrigible by good training from without and persistent moral effort from within) <u>to resent the existence of what is stronger, subtler or better than themselves</u>. In uncorrected and brutal men this hardens into an implacable and disinterested hatred for every kind of excellence. The vocabulary of a period tells tales. There is reason to be alarmed at the immense vogue today of such words as "high-brow," "up-stage," "old school tie," "academic," "smug," and "complacent." These words, as used today, are sores: one feels the poison throbbing in them.

Present Concerns

"I thought love meant equality," she said, "and free companionship."

"Ah, equality?" said the Director. "We must talk of that some other time. Yes, we must all be guarded by equal rights from one another's greed, because we are fallen. Just as we must all wear clothes for the same reason. But the naked body should be there underneath the clothes, ripening for the day when we shall need them no longer. <u>Equality is not the deepest thing, you know.</u>"

"I always thought that was just what it was. I thought it was in their souls that people were equal."

"You were mistaken," said he gravely. "That is the last place where they are equal. Equality before the law, equality of incomes—that is very well. Equality guards life; it doesn't make it. It is medicine, not food."

That Hideous Strength

EVANGELISM

Of course as priests it is the outsiders you will have to cope with. You exist in the long run for no other purpose. The proper study of shepherds is sheep, not (save accidentally) other shepherds. And woe to you if you do not evangelize.

Christian Reflections

You can't lay down any pattern for God. There are many different ways of bringing people into His Kingdom, even some ways that I specially dislike! I have therefore learned to be cautious in my judgment.

But we can block it in many ways. As Christians we are tempted to make unnecessary concessions to those outside the Faith. We give in too much. Now, I don't mean that we should run the risk of making a nuisance of ourselves by witnessing at improper times, but there comes a time when we must show that we disagree. We must show our Christian colours, if we are to be true to Jesus Christ. We cannot remain silent or concede everything away.

I turn now to the question of the actual attack. This may be either emotional or intellectual. If I speak only of the intellectual kind, that is not because I undervalue the other but because, not having been given the gifts necessary for carrying it out, I cannot give advice about it. But I wish to say most emphatically that where a speaker has that gift, the direct evangelical appeal of the "Come to Jesus" type can be as overwhelming today as it was a hundred years ago. I have seen it done, preluded by a religious

difference btwn the emotional + intellectual attack of evangelism. For me, it's intellectual. For Mom, it's emotional.

film and accompanied by hymn singing, and with very remarkable effect. I cannot do it: but those who can ought to do it with all their might. I am not sure that the ideal missionary team ought not to consist of one who argues and one who (in the fullest sense of the word) preaches. Put up your arguer first to undermine their intellectual prejudices; then let the evangelist proper launch his appeal. I have seen this done with great success.

God in the Dock

My feeling about people in whose conversion I have been allowed to play a part is always mixed with awe and even fear: such as a boy might feel on first being allowed to fire a rifle. The disproportion between his puny finger on the trigger and the thunder and lightening wh. follow is alarming. And the seriousness with which the other party takes my words always raises the doubt whether I have taken them seriously enough myself. By writing the things I write, you see, one especially qualifies for being hereafter "condemned out of one's own mouth." Think of me as a fellow-patient in the same hospital who, having been admitted a little earlier, cd. give some advice.

The Collected Letters of C. S. Lewis, Volume III

Good things as well as bad, you know, are caught by a kind of infection. If you want to get warm you must stand near the fire: if you want to be wet you must get into the water. If you want joy, power, peace, eternal life, you must get close to, or even into, the thing that has them. They are not a sort of prize which God could, if He chose, just hand out to anyone. They are a great fountain of energy and beauty spurting up at the very centre of reality. If you are close to it, the spray will wet you: if you are not, you will remain dry. Once a man is united to God, how could he not live forever?

Mere Christianity

EVIL

Badness cannot succeed even in being bad in the same way in which goodness is good. Goodness is, so to speak, itself: badness is only spoiled goodness.

But in reality we have no experience of anyone liking badness just because it is bad. The nearest we can get to it is in cruelty. But in real life people are cruel for one of two reasons—either because they are sadists, that is, because they have a sexual perversion which makes cruelty a cause of sensual pleasure to them, or else for the sake of something they are going to get out of it—money, or power, or safety. But pleasure, money, power, and safety are all, as far as they go, good things. The badness consists in pursuing them by the wrong method, or in the wrong way, or too much. I do not mean, of course, that the people who do this are not desperately wicked. I do mean that wickedness, when you examine it, turns out to be the pursuit of some good in the wrong way. . . . To be bad, [Satan] must exist and have intelligence and will. But existence, intelligence and will are in themselves good. Therefore he must be getting them from the Good Power: even to be bad he must borrow or steal from his opponent. And do you now begin to see why Christianity has always said that the devil is a fallen angel? That is not a mere story for the children. It is a real recognition of the fact that evil is a parasite, not an original thing. The powers which enable evil to carry on are powers given to it by goodness. All the things which enable a bad man to be effectively bad are in themselves good things—resolution, cleverness, good looks, existence itself. That is why Dualism, in a strict sense, will not work.

Mere Christianity

The greatest evil is not now done in those sordid "dens of crime" that Dickens loved to paint. It is not done even in concentration camps and labour camps. In those we see its final result. But it is conceived and ordered (moved, seconded, carried, and minuted) in clean, carpeted, warmed, and well-lighted offices, by quiet men with white collars and cut fingernails and smooth-shaven cheeks who do not need to raise their voice.

The Screwtape Letters, Preface

"You spoke yesterday, Lady, of clinging to the old good instead of taking the good that came."

"Yes—for a few heartbeats."

"There was an eldil [Satan] who clung longer—who has been clinging since before the worlds were made."

"But the old good would cease to be a good at all if he did that."

"Yes. It has ceased. And still he clings."

Perelandra

I think one may be quite rid of the old haunting suspicion—which raises its head in every temptation—that there is something else than God—some other country . . . into which He forbids us to trespass—some kind of delight wh. He "doesn't appreciate" or just chooses to forbid, but which wd. be real delight if only we were allowed to get it. The thing just isn't there. Whatever we desire is either what God is trying to give us as quickly as He can, or else a false picture of what He is trying to give us—a false picture wh. would not attract us for a moment if we saw the real thing. Therefore God does really in a sense contain evil—i.e., contains what is the real motive power behind all our evil desires. He knows what we want, even in our vilest acts: He is longing to give it to us. He is not looking on from the outside at some new "taste" or "separate desire of our own." Only because He has laid up real goods for us to desire are we able to go wrong by snatching at them in greedy, misdirected ways. The truth is that evil is not a real thing at all, like God. It is simply good spoiled. That is why I say there can be good without evil, but no evil without good. You know what the biologists mean by a parasite—an animal that lives on another animal. Evil is a parasite. It is there only because good is there for it to spoil and confuse.

Thus you may well feel that God understands our temptations—understands them a great deal more than we do. But don't forget Macdonald again—"Only God understands evil and hates it." Only the dog's master knows how useless it is to try to get on with the lead knotted round the lamp-post. This is why we must be prepared to find God implacably and immovably forbidding what may seem to us very small and trivial things. But He knows whether they are really small and trivial. How small some of the things that doctors forbid would seem to an ignoramus.

The Collected Letters of C. S. Lewis, Volume II

EXCUSES

The difference between this situation [forgiving others] and the
one in which you are asking God's forgiveness is this. In our own
case we accept our own excuses too easily, in other people's we do not
accept them easily enough. As regards my own sins it is a safe bet
(though not a certainty) that the excuses are not really so good
as I think; as regards other men's sins against me it is a safe bet
(though not a certainty) that the excuses are better than I think.

To excuse what can really produce good excuses is not Christian charity; it is only fairness. To be a Christian means to forgive
the inexcusable, because God has forgiven the inexcusable in you.

The Weight of Glory

EXPERIENCE

In all my life I have met only one person who claims to have seen a ghost. And the interesting thing about the story is that that person disbelieved in the immortal soul before she saw the ghost and still disbelieves after seeing it. She says that what she saw must have been an illusion or a trick of the nerves. And obviously she may be right. Seeing is not believing.

For this reason, the question whether miracles occur can never be answered simply by experience. Every event which might claim to be a miracle is, in the last resort, something presented to our senses, something seen, heard, touched, smelled, or tasted. And our senses are not infallible.

Miracles

"Religious experience" in the narrower sense comes and goes: especially goes. The operation of Faith is to retain, so far as the will and intellect are concerned, what is irresistible and obvious during the moments of special grace.

God in the Dock

[The demon Screwtape writes:] Experience, in the peculiar sense we teach them to give it, is, by the bye, a most useful word. A great human philosopher nearly let our secret out when he said that where Virtue is concerned "Experience is the mother of illusion"; but thanks to a change in Fashion, and also, of course, to the Historical Point of View, we have largely rendered his book innocuous.

The Screwtape Letters

FAILURE

No amount of falls will really undo us if we keep picking ourselves up each time. We shall of course be very muddy and tat-
tered children by the time we reach home. But the bathrooms are
all ready, the towels put out, & the clean clothes are in the airing
cupboard. The only fatal thing is to lose one's temper and give it
up. It is when we notice the dirt that God is most present in us; it
is the very sign of His presence.

The Collected Letters of C. S. Lewis, Volume II

At the moment, I can well imagine, everything seems in ruins.
That is an illusion. The world is full of capable and useful people
who began life by ploughing in exams. You will laugh at this *con-
tre temps* ["setback"] some day. Of course it wd. be disastrous
to go to the other extreme and conclude that one was a genius
because one had failed in a prelim—as if a horse imagined it must
be a Derby winner because it couldn't be taught to pull a four-
wheeler!—but I don't expect that is the extreme to which you are
temperamentally inclined.

Are you in any danger of seeking consolation in Resentment?
I have no reason to suppose you are, but it is a favourite desire of
the human mind (certainly of my mind!) and one wants to be on
one's guard against it. And that is about the only way in which
an early failure like this can become a real permanent injury. A
belief that one has been misused, a tendency ever after to snap
and snarl at "the system"—that, I think, makes a man always a

bore, usually an ass, sometimes a villain. So don't think either that you are no good or that you are a Victim. Write the whole thing off and get on.

You may reply "It's easy talking." I shan't blame you if you do. I remember only too well what a hopeless oyster to be opened the world seemed at your age. I would have given a good deal to anyone who cd. have assured me that I ever wd. be able to persuade anyone to pay me a living wage for anything I cd. do. Life consisted of applying for jobs which other people got, writing books that no one wd. publish, and giving lectures wh. no one attended. It all looks perfectly hopeless. Yet the vast majority of us manage to get in somewhere and shake down somehow in the end.

You are now going through what most people (at any rate most of the people I know) find in retrospect to have been the most unpleasant period of their lives. But it won't last: the road usually improves later. I think life is rather like a lumpy bed in a bad hotel. At first you can't imagine how you can lie on it, much less sleep in it. But presently one finds the right position and finally one is snoring away. By the time one is called it seems a v. good bed and one is loth to leave it.

A text you shd. keep much is mind is I John iii, 20: "If our heart condemns us God is greater than our heart." I sometimes pray "Lord give me no more and no less self-knowledge than I can at this moment make a good use of." Remember He is the artist and you are only the picture. You can't see it. So quietly submit to be painted—i.e., keep on fulfilling all the obvious duties of your station (you really know quite well enough what they are!), asking forgiveness for each failure and then leaving it alone. You are in the right way. Walk—don't keep on looking at it.

The Collected Letters of C. S. Lewis, Volume III

"Pray at this moment. Give me no more self-knowledge than I can make use of."

FAITH

It is a profound mistake to imagine that Christianity ever intended to dissipate the bewilderment and even the terror, the sense of our own nothingness, which come upon us when we think about the nature of things. It comes to intensify them. Without such sensations there is no religion. Many a man, brought up in the glib profession of some shallow form of Christianity, who comes through reading Astronomy to realise for the first time how majestically indifferent most reality is to man, and who perhaps abandons his religion on that account, may at that moment be having his first genuinely religious experience.

Miracles

Now Faith, in the sense in which I am here using the word, is the art of holding on to things your reason has once accepted, in spite of your changing moods. For moods will change, whatever view your reason takes. I know that by experience. Now that I am a Christian I do have moods in which the whole thing looks very improbable: but when I was an atheist I had moods in which Christianity looked terribly probable. This rebellion of your moods against your real self is going to come anyway. That is why Faith is such a necessary virtue: unless you teach your moods "where they get off," you can never be either a sound Christian or even a sound atheist, but just a creature dithering to and fro, with its beliefs really dependent on the weather and the state of its digestion. Consequently one must train the habit of Faith.

Mere Christianity

I suppose living from day to day ("take no thought for the morrow") is precisely what we have to "larn"—though the Old Adam in me sometimes murmurs that if God wanted me to live like the lilies of the field, I wonder He didn't give me the same lack of nerves and imagination as they enjoy! Or is that just the point, the precise purpose of this Divine paradox and audacity called Man—to do with a mind what other organisms do without it?

The Collected Letters of C. S. Lewis, Volume III

[The demon Screwtape writes:] Do not be deceived, Wormwood. Our cause is never more in danger than when a human, no longer desiring, but still intending, to do our Enemy's will, looks round upon a universe from which every trace of Him seems to have vanished, and asks why he has been forsaken, and still obeys.

The Screwtape Letters

FAITH AND WORKS

I take it as a first principle that we must not interpret any one part of Scripture so that it contradicts other parts, and specially we must not use an apostle's teaching to contradict that of Our Lord. Whatever St. Paul may have meant, we must not reject the parable of the sheep and the goats. There, you see there is nothing about Predestination, or even about Faith—all depends on works. But how this is to be reconciled with St. Paul's teaching, or with other sayings of Our Lord, I frankly confess I don't know. Even St. Peter you know admits that he was stumped by the Pauline Epistles (II Peter, iii 16–17).

What I think is this. Everyone looking back on his own conversion must feel—and I am sure the feeling is in some sense true— "It is not I who have done this. I did not choose Christ: He chose me. It is all free grace, wh. I have done nothing to earn." That is the Pauline account: and I am sure it is the only true account of every conversion from the inside. Very well. It then seems to us logical & natural to turn this personal experience into a general rule, "All conversions depend on God's choice."

But this I believe is exactly what we must not do: for generalisations are legitimate only when we are dealing with matters to which our faculties are adequate. Here, we are not. How our individual experiences are in reality consistent with (a) Our idea of Divine justice, (b) The parable I've just quoted & lots of other passages, we don't & can't know: what is clear is that we can't find a consistent formula. I think we must take a leaf out of the scientists' book. They are quite familiar with the fact that, for example, Light has to be regarded both as a wave in the ether and as a stream of particles. No one can make these two views consistent. Of course reality must be self-consistent: but till (if ever) we can see the consistency it is better to hold two inconsistent views than to ignore one side of the evidence.

The real inter-relation between God's omnipotence and Man's freedom is something we can't find out. Looking at the Sheep & the Goats every man can be quite sure that every kind act he does will be accepted by Christ. Yet, equally, we all do feel sure that all the good in us comes from Grace. We have to leave it at that. I find the best plan is to take the Calvinist view of my own virtues and other people's vices: and the other view of my own vices and other people's virtues. But tho' there is much to be puzzled about, there is nothing to be worried about. It is plain from Scripture that, in whatever sense the Pauline doctrine is true, it is not true in any sense which excludes its (apparent) opposite.

You know what Luther said: "Do you doubt if you are chosen? Then say your prayers and you may conclude that you are."

The Collected Letters of C. S. Lewis, Volume III

And on the purely theological level I think I may say that the barrier is no longer that between a doctrine of Faith and a doctrine of Works. I am not myself convinced that any good Roman [Catholic] ever did hold the doctrine of Works in that form of which Protestants accused him, or that any good Protestant ever did hold the doctrine of Faith in that form of which Romans accused him.

C. S. Lewis: Essay Collection and Other Short Pieces

FAITHFULNESS

plans are made. While I can, I sail east in the *Dawn*
When she fails me, I paddle east in my coracle. When she
shall swim east with my four paws. And when I can swim
nger, if I have not reached Aslan's country, or shot over the
of the world in some vast cataract, I shall sink with my nose
the sunrise and Reepicheep will be head of the talking mice in
arnia."

The Voyage of the DAWN TREADER

THE FALL

I am a democrat because I believe in the Fall of Man. I think
most people are democrats for the opposite reason. A great deal
of democratic enthusiasm descends from the ideas of people like
Rousseau, who believed in democracy because they thought mankind so wise and good that everyone deserved a share in the gov-
ernment. The danger of defending democracy on those grounds
is that they're not true. And whenever their weakness is exposed,
the people who prefer tyranny make capital out of the exposure. I
find that they're not true without looking further than myself. I
don't deserve a share in governing a hen-roost, much less a nation.
Nor do most people: all the people who believe advertisements,
and think in catchwords and spread rumours. The real reason for
democracy is just the reverse. Mankind is so fallen that no man
can be trusted with unchecked power over his fellows. Aristotle
said that some people were only fit to be slaves. I do not contradict him. But I reject slavery because I see no men fit to be
masters.

Present Concerns

The doctrine of the Fall (both of man and of some "gods," "eldils"
or "angels") is the only satisfactory explanation. Evil begins, in a
universe where all was good, from free will, which was permitted
because it makes possible the greatest good of all. The corruption
of the first sinner consists not in choosing some evil thing (there
are no evil things for him to choose) but in preferring a lesser

good (himself) before a greater (God). The Fall is, in fact, Pride. The possibility of this wrong preference is inherent in the v. fact of having, or being, a self at all. But though freedom is real it is not infinite. Every choice reduces a little one's freedom to choose the next time. There therefore comes a time when the creature is fully built, irrevocably attached either to God or to itself. This irrevocableness is what we call Heaven or Hell. Every conscious agent is finally committed in the long run: i.e., it rises above freedom into willed, but henceforth unalterable, union with God, or else sinks below freedom into the black fire of self-imprisonment. That is why the universe (as even the physicists now admit) has a real history, a fifth act with a finale in which the good characters "live happily ever after" and the bad ones are cast out. At least that is how I see it.

The Collected Letters of C. S. Lewis, Volume II

[Mother Kirk's Story:] "You must know that once upon a time there were no tenants in this country at all, for the Landlord used to farm it himself. There were only the animals and the Landlord used to look after them, he and his sons and daughters. Every morning they used to come down from the mountains and milk the cows and lead out the sheep to pasture. And they needed less watching, for all the animals were tamer then; and there were no fences needed, for if a wolf got in among the flocks he would do them no harm. And one day the Landlord was going home from his day's work when he looked round on the country, and the beasts, and saw how the crops were springing, and it came into his head that the whole thing was too good to keep to himself.

So he decided to let the country to tenants, and his first tenant was a young married man. But first the Landlord made a farm in the very centre of the land where the soil was the best and the air most wholesome, and that was the very spot where you are sitting now. They were to have the whole land, but that was too much for them to keep under cultivation. The Landlord's idea was that they could work the farm and leave the rest as a park for the time being: but later they could divide the park up into holdings for their children. For you must know that he drew up a very different lease from the kind you have nowadays. It was a lease in perpetuity on his side, for he promised never to turn them out; but on their side, they could leave when they chose, as long as one of their sons was there, to take the farm on, and then they could go up to live with him in the mountains. He thought that would be a good thing because it would broaden the minds of his own mountain children to mix with strangers. And they thought so too. But before he put the tenants in possession there was one thing he had to do. Up to this time the country had been full of a certain fruit which the Landlord had planted for the refreshment of himself and his children, if they were thirsty during the day as they worked down here. It was a very good fruit and up in the mountains they say it is even more plentiful: but it is very strong and only those who are mountain-bred ought to eat it, for only they can digest it properly. Hitherto, while there were only beasts in the land, it had done no harm for these mountain-apples to be growing in every thicket; for you know that an animal will eat nothing but what it is good for it. But now that there were to be men in the land, the Landlord was afraid that they might do themselves an injury; yet it was not to be thought of that he should dig up every sapling of that tree and make the country into a desert. So he decided that it was best to be frank with the young people, and when he found a great big mountain-apple tree growing in the very centre of the farm he said, "So much the better. If they are to learn sense, they may as well learn it from the beginning: and if they will not, there's no help for it. For if they did not find mountain-apples on the farm, they would soon find them somewhere else." So he left the apple tree standing, and put the man and his wife into their farm: but before he left them he explained the whole affair to them—as much of it could be explained—and warned them on no account to eat any of the apples. Then he went home. And for a time the young man and his wife behaved very well, tending the animals and managing their farm, and abstaining from the mountain-apples; and for all I know they might never have done otherwise if the wife had not somehow made a new acquaintance. This new acquaintance was a landowner himself. He had been born in the mountains and was one of our Landlord's own children, but he had quarrelled with his father and set up on his own, and now had built up a very considerable estate in another country. His estate marches, however, with this country: and as he was a great land-grabber he always wanted to take this bit in—and he has very nearly succeeded."

"I've never met any tenants of his," said John.

"Not tenants in chief, my dear," said the old woman. "And so you didn't know them. But you may have met the Clevers, who are tenants of Mr. Mammon: and he is a tenant of the Spirit of the Age: who holds directly of the Enemy."

"I am sure the Clevers would be very surprised," said John, "to hear that they had a Landlord at all. They would think this enemy, as you call him, no less a superstition than your Landlord."

"But that is how business is managed," said Mother Kirk. "The little people do not know the big people to whom they belong. The big people do not intend that they should. No important transference of property could be carried out if all the small people at the bottom knew what was really happening. But this is not part of my story. As I was saying, the enemy got to know the farmer's wife: and, however he did it, or whatever he said to her, it wasn't long before he persuaded her that the one thing she needed was a nice mountain-apple. And she took one and ate it. And then—you know how it is with husbands—she made the farmer come round to her mind. And at the moment he put out his hand and plucked the fruit there was an earthquake, and the country cracked open all the way across from North to South: and ever since, instead of the farm, there has been this gorge, which the country people call the Grand Canyon. But in my language its name is Peccatum Adae ["The Sin of Adam"]."

The Pilgrim's Regress

FAMILY

The grandfather, the parents, the grown-up son, the child, the dog, and the cat are true members [of the family] (in the organic sense) precisely because they are not members or units of a homogeneous class. They are not interchangeable. Each person is almost a species in himself. The mother is not simply a different person from the daughter, she is a different kind of person. The grown-up brother is not simply one unit in the class children, he is a separate estate of the realm. The father and grandfather are almost as different as the cat and the dog. If you subtract any one member you have not simply reduced the family in number, you have inflicted an injury on its structure. Its unity is a unity of unlikes, almost of incommensurables.

The Weight of Glory

FASTING

Perhaps if we had done more voluntary fasting before, God would not now have put us on these darn diets! Well, the theologians say that an imposed mortification can have all the merit of a voluntary one if it is taken in the right spirit.

The Collected Letters of C. S. Lewis, Volume III

The problem about avoiding our own pain admits a similar solution. Some ascetics have used self-torture. As a layman, I offer no opinion on the prudence of such a regimen; but I insist that, whatever its merits, self-torture is quite a different thing from tribulation sent by God. Everyone knows that fasting is a different experience from missing your dinner by accident or through poverty. Fasting asserts the will against the appetite—the reward being self-mastery and the danger pride: involuntary hunger subjects appetites and will together to the Divine will, furnishing an occasion for submission and exposing us to the danger of rebellion. But the redemptive effect of suffering lies chiefly in its tendency to reduce the rebel will. Ascetic practices, which in themselves strengthen the will, are only useful in so far as they enable the will to put its own house (the passions) in order, as a preparation for offering the whole man to God. They are necessary as a means; as an end, they would be abominable, for in substituting will for appetite and there stopping, they would merely exchange the animal self for the diabolical self.

The Problem of Pain

FEAR

Even in real life different kinds of danger produce different kinds of fear. There may come a point at which fear is so great that such distinctions vanish, but that is another matter. There is a fear which is twin sister to awe, such as a man in war-time feels when he first comes within sound of the guns; there is a fear which is twin sister to disgust, such as a man feels on finding a snake or scorpion in his bedroom. There are taut, quivering fears (for one split second hardly distinguishable from a kind of pleasurable thrill) that a man may feel on a dangerous horse or a dangerous sea; and again, dead, squashed, flattened, numbing fears, as when we think we have cancer or cholera. There are also fears which are not of danger at all: like the fear of some large and hideous, though innocuous, insect or the fear of a ghost. All this, even in real life. But in imagination, where the fear does not rise to abject terror and is not discharged in action, the qualitative difference is much stronger.

C. S. Lewis on Stories

Perfect love, we know, casteth out fear. But so do several other things—ignorance, alcohol, passion, presumption, and stupidity. It is very desirable that we should all advance to that perfection of love in which we shall fear no longer; but it is very undesirable, until we have reached that stage, that we should allow any inferior agent to cast out our fear.

The World's Last Night

Those who say that children must not be frightened may mean two things. They may mean (1) that we must not do anything likely to give the child those haunting, disabling, pathological fears against which ordinary courage is helpless: in fact, phobias. His mind must, if possible, be kept clear of things he can't bear to think of. Or they may mean (2) that we must try to keep out of his mind the knowledge that he is born into a world of death, violence, wounds, adventure, heroism and cowardice, good and evil. If they mean the first I agree with them: but not if they mean the second. The second would indeed be to give children a false impression and feed them on escapism in the bad sense. There is something ludicrous in the idea of so educating a generation which is born to the Ogpu and the atomic bomb. Since it is so likely that they will meet cruel enemies, let them at least have heard of brave knights and heroic courage. Otherwise you are making their destiny not brighter but darker. Nor do most of us find that violence and bloodshed, in a story, produce any haunting dread in the minds of children. As far as that goes, I side impenitently with the human race against the modern reformer. Let there be wicked kings and beheadings, battles and dungeons, giants and dragons, and let villains be soundly killed at the end of the book. Nothing will persuade me that this causes an ordinary child any kind or degree of fear beyond what it wants, and needs, to feel. For, of course, it wants to be a little frightened.

C. S. Lewis on Stories

FEELING

I think the thrill of the Pagan stories and of romance may be due to the fact that they are mere beginnings—the first, faint whisper of the wind from beyond the world—while Christianity is the thing itself: and no thing, when you have really started on it, can have for you then and there just the same thrill as the first hint. For example, the experience of being married and bringing up a family cannot have the old bittersweet of first falling in love. But it is futile (and, I think, wicked) to go on trying to get the old thrill again: you must go forward and not backward. Any real advance will in its turn be ushered in by a new thrill, different from the old: doomed in its turn to disappear and to become in its turn a temptation to retrogression. Delight is a bell that rings as you set your foot on the first step of a new flight of stairs leading upwards. Once you have started climbing you will notice only the hard work: it is when you have reached the landing and catch sight of the new stair that you may expect the bell again. This is only an idea, and may be all rot: but it seems to fit in pretty well with the general law (thrills also must die to live) of autumn & spring, sleep and waking, death and resurrection, and "Whosoever loseth his life, shall save it."

The Collected Letters of C. S. Lewis, Volume II

And of course the presence of God is not the same as the sense of the presence of God. The latter may be due to imagination; the former may be attended with no "sensible consolation." The

Father was not really absent from the Son when He said "Why hast thou forsaken me?" You see God Himself, as man, submitted to man's sense of being abandoned. The real parallel on the natural level is one which seems odd for a bachelor to write to a lady, but too illuminating not to be used. The act which engenders a child ought to be, and usually is attended by pleasure. But it is not the pleasure that produces the child. Where there is pleasure there may be sterility: where there is no pleasure the act may be fertile. And in the spiritual marriage of God and the soul it is the same. It is the actual presence, not the sensation of the presence, of the Holy Ghost which begets Christ in us. The sense of the presence is a super-added gift for which we give thanks when it comes, and that's all about it.

The Collected Letters of C. S. Lewis, Volume III

"Yes," said the Director. "There is no escape. If it were a virginal rejection of the male, He would allow it. Such souls can bypass the male and go on to meet something far more masculine, higher up, to which they must make a yet deeper surrender. But your trouble has been what old poets called Daungier. We call it Pride. You are offended by the masculine itself: the loud, irruptive, possessive thing—the gold lion, the bearded bull—which breaks through hedges and scatters the little kingdom of your primness as the dwarfs scattered the carefully made bed. The male you could have escaped, for it exists only on the biological level. But the masculine none of us can escape. What is above and beyond all things is so masculine that we are all feminine in relation to it. You had better agree with your adversary quickly."

That Hideous Strength

At all events what Ransom saw at that moment was the real meaning of gender. Everyone must sometimes have wondered why in nearly all tongues certain inanimate objects are masculine and others feminine. What is masculine about a mountain or feminine about certain trees? Ransom has cured me of believing that this is a purely morphological phenomenon, depending on the form of the word. Still less is gender an imaginative extension of sex. Our ancestors did not make mountains masculine because they projected male characteristics into them. The real process is the reverse. Gender is a reality, and a more fundamental reality than sex. Sex is, in fact, merely the adaptation to organic life of a fundamental polarity which divides all created beings. Female sex is simply one of the things that have feminine gender; there are many others, and Masculine and Feminine meet us on planes of reality where male and female would be simply meaningless. Masculine is not attenuated male, nor feminine attenuated female. On the contrary, the male and female of organic creatures are rather faint and blurred reflections of masculine and feminine. Their reproductive functions, their differences in strength and size, partly exhibit, but partly also confuse and misrepresent, the real polarity. All this Ransom saw, as it were, with his own eyes. The two white creatures were sexless. But he of Malacandra was masculine (not male); she of Perelandra was feminine (not female).

Perelandra

For a good wife contains so many persons in herself. What was H. not to me? She was my daughter and my mother, my pupil and my teacher, my subject and my sovereign; and always, holding all these in solution, my trusty comrade, friend, shipmate, fellow-soldier. My mistress; but at the same time all that any man friend (and I have good ones) has ever been to me. Perhaps more. If we had never fallen in love we should have none the less been always together, and created a scandal. That's what I meant when I once praised her for her "masculine virtues." But she soon put a stop to that by asking how I'd like to be praised for my feminine ones. It was a good riposte, dear. Yet there was something of the Amazon, something of Penthesileia and Camilla. And you, as well as I, were glad it should be there. You were glad I should recognize it.

Solomon calls his bride Sister. Could a woman be a complete wife unless, for a moment, in one particular mood, a man felt almost inclined to call her Brother? . . .

There is, hidden or flaunted, a sword between the sexes till an entire marriage reconciles them. It is arrogance in us to call frankness, fairness, and chivalry "masculine" when we see them in a woman; it is arrogance in them to describe a man's sensitiveness or tact or tenderness as "feminine." But also what poor, warped fragments of humanity most mere men and mere women must be to make the implications of that arrogance plausible. Marriage heals this. Jointly the two become fully human. "In the image of God created He them." Thus, by a paradox, this carnival of sexuality leads us out beyond our sexes.

A Grief Observed

FORGIVENESS

I find that when I think I am asking God to forgive me I am often in reality (unless I watch myself very carefully) asking Him to do something quite different. I am asking Him not to forgive me but to excuse me. But there is all the difference in the world between forgiving and excusing. Forgiveness says "Yes, you have done this thing, but I accept your apology, I will never hold it against you and everything between us two will be exactly as it was before." But excusing says "I see that you couldn't help it or didn't mean it, you weren't really to blame.". . .

Real forgiveness means looking steadily at the sin, the sin that is left over without any excuse, after all allowances have been made, and seeing it in all its horror, dirt, meanness and malice, and nevertheless being wholly reconciled to the man who has done it.

The Weight of Glory

It's the mixture, or alternation, of resentment and affection that is so very uneasy, isn't it? For the indulgence of either immediately comes slap up against the other, which then, a few seconds later comes slap up against it, so that the mind does a diabolical "shuttle-service" to and fro between them. We've all at some time in our lives, I expect, had this experience. Except possibly anxiety nothing is more hostile to sleep. One must try, I suppose, to keep on remembering that the love part of the suffering is good and purgatorial while the anger part is bad and infernal.

Yet how madly one cherishes that base part as if it were one's dearest possession—dwells on everything that can aggravate the offence—and keeps on thinking of things one wd. like to say to the other party! I suppose all one can do is to keep on meditating on the petition "Forgive us our trespasses as we forgive those that trespass against us."

I find Fear a great help—the fear that my own unforgivingness will exclude me from all the promises. Fear tames wrath. And this fear (we have Our Lord's word for it) is wholly well-grounded. The human heart (mine anyway) is "desperately wicked." Joy often quoted this in connection with the great difficulty she found in forgiving a v. near and v. nasty relative of her own. One has to keep on doing it over again, doesn't one?

As for myself, during the past year a great joy has befallen me. Difficult though it is, I shall try to explain this in words. It is astonishing that sometimes we believe that we believe what, really, in our heart, we do not believe. For a long time I believed that I believed in the forgiveness of sins. But suddenly this truth appeared in my mind in so clear a light that I perceived that never before (and that after many confessions and absolutions) had I believed it with my whole heart.

Do you know, only a few weeks ago I realised suddenly that I at last had forgiven the cruel schoolmaster who so darkened my childhood. I'd been trying to do it for years; and like you, each time I thought I'd done it, I found, after a week or so it all had to be attempted over again. But this time I feel sure it is the real thing. And (like learning to swim or to ride a bicycle) the moment it does happen it seems so easy and you wonder why on earth you didn't do it years ago. So the parable of the unjust judge comes true, and what has been vainly asked for years can suddenly be granted. I also get a quite new feeling about "If you forgive you will be forgiven." I don't believe it is, as it sounds, a bargain. The forgiving and the being forgiven are really the very same thing. But one is safe as long as one keeps on trying.

The Collected Letters of C. S. Lewis, Volume III

Love may forgive all infirmities and love still in spite of them: but Love cannot cease to will their removal.

The Problem of Pain

FREEDOM (AND PREDESTINATION)

Witness the doctrine of Predestination which shows (truly enough) that eternal reality is not waiting for a future in which to be real; but at the price of removing Freedom which is the deeper truth of the two.

The Great Divorce

All that Calvinist question—Free-Will & Predestination, is to my mind undiscussable, insoluble. Of course (say us) if a man repents God will accept him. Ah yes (say they), but the fact of his repenting shows that God has already moved him to do so. This at any rate leaves us with the fact that in any concrete case the question never arrives as a practical one. But I suspect it is really a meaningless question. The difference between Freedom & Necessity is fairly clear on the bodily level: we know the difference between making our teeth chatter on purpose & just finding them chattering with cold. It begins to be less clear when we talk of human love (leaving out the erotic kind). "Do I like him because I choose or because I must?"—there are cases where this has an answer, but others where it seems to me to mean nothing. When we carry it up to relations between God & Man, has the distinction perhaps become nonsensical? After all, when we are most free, it is only with a freedom God has given us: and when our will is most influenced by Grace, it is still our will. And if what our will does is not "voluntary," and if "voluntary" does not mean "free," what are we talking about? I'd leave it all alone.

The Collected Letters of C. S. Lewis, Volume III

I was not born to be free—I was born to adore and obey.

C. S. Lewis at the Breakfast Table and Other Reminiscences

It will be too late then to choose your side. There is no use saying you choose to lie down when it has become impossible to stand up. That will not be the time for choosing: it will be the time when we discover which side we really have chosen, whether we realised it before or not. Now, today, this moment, is our chance to choose the right side. God is holding back to give us that chance. It will not last for ever. We must take it or leave it.

Every time you make a choice you are turning the central part of you, the part of you that chooses, into something a little different from what it was before. And taking your life as a whole, with all your innumerable choices, all your life long you are slowly turning this central thing either into a heavenly creature or into a hellish creature: either into a creature that is in harmony with God, and with other creatures, and with itself, or else into one that is in a state of war and hatred with God, and with its fellow-creatures, and with itself. To be the one kind of creature is heaven: that is, it is joy and peace and knowledge and power. To be the other means madness, horror, idiocy, rage, impotence, and eternal loneliness. Each of us at each moment is progressing to the one state or the other.

Mere Christianity

From the moment a creature becomes aware of God as God and of itself as self, the terrible alternative of choosing God or self for the centre is opened to it.

The Problem of Pain

Heaven will solve our problems, but not, I think, by showing us subtle reconciliations between all our apparently contradictory notions. The notions will all be knocked from under our feet. We shall see that there never was any problem.

A Grief Observed

FREE WILL

The sin, both of men and of angels, was rendered possible by the fact that God gave them free will: this surrendering a portion of His omnipotence (it is again a deathlike or descending movement) because He saw that from a world of free creatures, even though they fell, He could work out (and this is the re-ascent) a deeper happiness and a fuller splendour than any world of automata would admit.

Miracles

You will notice that Scripture just sails over the problem [of grace and free will]. "Work out your own salvation in fear and trembling"—pure Pelagianism. But why? "For it is God who worketh in you"—pure Augustinianism.

Letters to Malcolm: Chiefly on Prayer

God created things which had free will. That means creatures which can go either wrong or right. Some people think they can imagine a creature which was free but had no possibility of going wrong; I cannot. If a thing is free to be good it is also free to be bad. And free will is what has made evil possible. Why, then, did God give them free will? Because free will, though it makes evil possible, is also the only thing that makes possible any love or goodness or joy worth having. A world of automata—of creatures that worked like machines—would hardly be worth creating. The happiness which God designs for His higher creatures is the happiness of being freely, voluntarily united to Him and to each other in an ecstasy of love and delight compared with which the most rapturous love between a man and a woman on this earth is mere milk and water. And for that they must be free.

Of course God knew what would happen if they used their freedom the wrong way: apparently He thought it worth the risk. Perhaps we feel inclined to disagree with Him. But there is a difficulty about disagreeing with God. He is the source from which all your reasoning power comes: you could not be right and He wrong any more than a stream can rise higher than its own source. When you are arguing against Him you are arguing against the very power that makes you able to argue at all: it is like cutting off the branch you are sitting on. If God thinks this state of war in the universe a price worth paying for free will—that is, for making a live world in which creatures can do real good or harm and something of real importance can happen, instead of a toy world which only moves when He pulls the strings—then we may take it it is worth paying.

Mere Christianity

FRIENDSHIP

In a perfect Friendship this Appreciative love is, I think, often so great and so firmly based that each member of the circle feels, in his secret heart, humbled before all the rest. Sometimes he wonders what he is doing there among his betters. He is lucky beyond desert to be in such company. Especially when the whole group is together, each bringing out all that is best, wisest, or funniest in all the others. Those are the golden sessions; when four or five of us after a hard day's walking have come to our inn; when our slippers are on, our feet spread out towards the blaze and our drinks at our elbows; when the whole world, and something beyond the world, opens itself to our minds as we talk; and no one has any claim on or any responsibility for another, but all are freemen and equals as if we had first met an hour ago, while at the same time an Affection mellowed by the years enfolds us. Life—natural life—has no better gift to give. Who could have deserved it?

The Four Loves

Are not all lifelong friendships born at the moment when at last you meet another human being who has some inkling (but faint and uncertain even in the best) of that something which you were born desiring, and which, beneath the flux of other desires and in all the momentary silences between the louder passions, night and day, year by year, from childhood to old age, you are looking for, watching for, listening for?

The Problem of Pain

Friendship exhibits a glorious "nearness by resemblance" to Heaven itself where the very multitude of the blessed (which no man can number) increases the fruition which each has of God. For every soul, seeing Him in her own way, doubtless communicates that unique vision to all the rest. That, says an old author, is why the Seraphim in Isaiah's vision are crying "Holy, Holy, Holy" to one another (Isaiah VI, 3). The more we thus share the Heavenly Bread between us, the more we shall all have.

The Four Loves

GLORY

[And this brings me to] the other sense of glory—glory as brightness, splendour, luminosity. We are to shine as the sun, we are to be given the Morning Star. I think I begin to see what it means. In one way, of course, God has given us the Morning Star already: you can go and enjoy the gift on many fine mornings if you get up early enough. What more, you may ask, do we want? Ah, but we want so much more—something the books on aesthetics take little notice of. But the poets and the mythologies know all about it. We do not want merely to see beauty, though, God knows, even that is bounty enough. We want something else which can hardly be put into words—to be united with the beauty we see, to pass into it, to receive it into ourselves, to bathe in it, to become part of it. That is why we have peopled air and earth and water with gods and goddesses and nymphs and elves—that, though we cannot, yet these projections can enjoy in themselves that beauty, grace, and power of which Nature is the image. That is why the poets tell us such lovely falsehoods. They talk as if the west wind could really sweep into a human soul; but it can't. They tell us that "beauty born of murmuring sound" will pass into a human face; but it won't. Or not yet. For if we take the imagery of Scripture seriously, if we believe that God will one day give us the Morning Star and cause us to put on the splendour of the sun, then we may surmise that both the ancient myths and the modern poetry, so false as history, may be very near the truth as prophecy. At present we are on the outside of the world, the wrong side of the door. We discern the freshness and purity of morning, but they do not make us fresh and pure. We cannot mingle with the splendours we see. But all the leaves of the New Testament are rustling with the rumour that it will not always be so. Some day, God willing, we shall get in. When human souls have become as perfect in voluntary obedience as the inanimate creation is in its lifeless obedience, then they will put on its glory, or rather that greater glory of which Nature is only the first sketch.

The Weight of Glory

GOD

As a great Christian writer (George MacDonald) pointed out, every father is pleased at the baby's first attempt to walk: no father would be satisfied with anything less than a firm, free, manly walk in a grown-up son. In the same way, he said, "God is easy to please, but hard to satisfy."

I think every one who has some vague belief in God, until he becomes a Christian, has the idea of an exam or of a bargain in his mind. The first result of real Christianity is to blow that idea into bits. When they find it blown into bits, some people think this means that Christianity is a failure and give up. They seem to imagine that God is very simple-minded! In fact, of course, He knows all about this. One of the very things Christianity was designed to do was to blow this idea to bits. God has been waiting for the moment at which you discover that there is no question of earning a pass mark in this exam or putting Him in your debt.

Then comes another discovery. Every faculty you have, your power of thinking or of moving your limbs from moment to moment, is given you by God. If you devoted every moment of your whole life exclusively to His service you could not give Him anything that was not in a sense His own already. So that when we talk of a man doing anything for God or giving anything to God, I will tell you what it is really like. It is like a small child going to his father and saying, "Daddy, give me sixpence to buy you a birthday present." Of course, the father does, and he is pleased with the child's present. It is all very nice and proper, but only an idiot would think that the father is sixpence to the good on the transaction. When a man has made these two discoveries God can really get to work. It is after this that real life begins.

Mere Christianity

God is Goodness. He can give good, but cannot need or get it. In that sense all His love is, as it were, bottomlessly selfless by very definition; it has everything to give and nothing to receive. Hence, if God sometimes speaks as though the Impassible could suffer passion and eternal fullness could be in want, and in want of those beings on whom it bestows all from their bare existence upwards, this can mean only, if it means anything intelligible by us, that God of mere miracle has made Himself able so to hunger and created in Himself that which we can satisfy. If He requires us, the requirement is of His own choosing.

It is a poor thing to strike our colours to God when the ship is going down under us; a poor thing to come to Him as a last resort, to offer up "our own" when it is no longer worth keeping. If God were proud He would hardly have us on such terms: but He is not proud, He stoops to conquer, He will have us even though we have shown that we prefer everything else to Him.

The Problem of Pain

It is always shocking to meet life where we thought we were alone. "Look out!" we cry, "it's alive." And therefore this is the very point at which so many draw back—I would have done so myself if I could—and proceed no further with Christianity. An "impersonal God"—well and good. A subjective God of beauty, truth and goodness, inside our own heads—better still. A formless life-force surging through us, a vast power which we can tap—best of all. But God Himself, alive, pulling at the other end of the cord, perhaps approaching at an infinite speed, the hunter, king, husband—that is quite another matter. There comes a moment when the children who have been playing at burglars hush suddenly: was that a real footstep in the hall? There comes a moment when people who have been dabbling in religion ("Man's search for God"!) suddenly draw back. Supposing we really found Him? We never meant it to come to that! Worse still, supposing He had found us! *"You would not have been calling to me unless I had been calling to you."*

Miracles

"Safe?" said Mr. Beaver. "Who said anything about safe? 'Course he isn't safe. But he's good. He's the King, I tell you."

The Lion, the Witch and the Wardrobe

He who has God and everything else has no more than he who has God only.

The Weight of Glory

Much of our backwardness in prayer is no doubt due to our sins, as every teacher will tell us; to our avoidable immersion in the things of this world, to our neglect of mental discipline. And also to the very worst kind of "fear of God." We shrink from too naked a contact, because we are afraid of the divine demands upon us which it might make too audible. As some old writer says, many a Christian prays faintly "lest God might really hear him, which he, poor man, never intended."

Letters to Malcolm: Chiefly on Prayer

"Hush!" said the other four, for now Aslan had stopped and turned and stood facing them, looking so majestic that they felt as glad as anyone can who feels afraid, and as afraid as anyone can who feels glad.

Prince Caspian

"Are you not thirsty?" said the Lion.

"I'm dying of thirst," said Jill.

"Then drink," said the Lion.

"May I—could I—would you mind going away while I do?" said Jill.

The Lion answered this only by a look and a very low growl. And as Jill gazed at its motionless bulk, she realised that she might as well have asked the whole mountain to move aside for her convenience.

The delicious rippling noise of the stream was driving her nearly frantic.

"Will you promise not to—do anything to me, if I do come?" said Jill.

"I make no promise," said the Lion.

Jill was so thirsty now that, without noticing it, she had come a step nearer.

"Do you eat girls?" she said.

"I have swallowed up girls and boys, women and men, kings and emperors, cities and realms," said the Lion. It didn't say this as if it were boasting, nor as if it were sorry, nor as if it were angry. It just said it.

"I daren't come and drink," said Jill.

"Then you will die of thirst," said the Lion.

"Oh dear!" said Jill, coming another step nearer. "I suppose I must go and look for another stream then."

"There is no other stream," said the Lion.

It never occurred to Jill to disbelieve the Lion, no one who had seen his stern face could do that—and her mind suddenly made itself up. It was the worst thing she had ever had to do, but she went forward to the stream, knelt down, and began scooping up water in her hand. It was the coldest, most refreshing water she had ever tasted. You didn't need to drink much of it, for it quenched your thirst at once. Before she tasted it she had been intending to make a dash away from the Lion the moment she had finished. Now, she realised that this would be on the whole the most dangerous thing of all.

The Silver Chair

God whispers to us in our pleasures, speaks in our conscience, but shouts in our pains: it is His megaphone to rouse a deaf world.

The Problem of Pain

The voice of God indeed daily calls to us; calls to the world to abandon sins and seek the Kingdom of God wholeheartedly.

O that we may all hear the call of the Father and, sometime, at last be converted to the Lord. . . . In silence and in meditation on the eternal truths, I hear the voice of God which excites our hearts to greater love.

The Collected Letters of C. S. Lewis, Volume II

GOODNESS

But it might be permissible to lay down two negations: that
God neither obeys nor creates the moral law. The good is uncreated; it never could have been otherwise; it has in it no shadow
of contingency; it lies, as Plato said, on the other side of existence. It is the Rita of the Hindus by which the gods themselves
are divine, the Tao of the Chinese from which all realities proceed. But we, favoured beyond the wisest pagans, know what lies
beyond existence, what admits no contingency, what lends divinity to all else, what is the ground of all existence, is not simply
a law but also a begetting love, a love begotten, and the love
which, being between these two, is also imminent in all those
who are caught up to share the unity of their self-caused life.
God is not merely good, but goodness; goodness is not merely
divine, but God.

Christian Reflections

It has sometimes been asked whether God commands certain
things because they are right, or whether certain things are right
because God commands them. . . . I emphatically embrace the
first alternative. The second might lead to the abominable conclu-
sion . . . that charity is good only because God arbitrarily commanded it—that He might equally well have commanded us to
hate Him and one another and that hatred would then have been
right. I believe, on the contrary, that "they err who think that
of the will of God to do this or that there is no reason besides

His will." God's will is determined by His wisdom which always perceives, and His goodness which always embraces, the intrinsically good. But when we have said that God commands things only because they are good, we must add that one of the things intrinsically good is that rational creatures should freely surrender themselves to their Creator in obedience. The content of our obedience—the thing we are commanded to do—will always be something intrinsically good, something we ought to do even if (by an impossible supposition) God had not commanded it. But in addition to the content, the mere obeying is also intrinsically good, for, in obeying, a rational creature consciously enacts its creaturely role, reverses the act by which we fell, treads Adam's dance backward, and returns.

The Problem of Pain

Good and evil both increase at compound interest. That is why the little decisions you and I make every day are of such infinite importance. The smallest good act today is the capture of a strategic point from which, a few months later, you may be able to go on to victories you never dreamed of. An apparently trivial indulgence in lust or anger today is the loss of a ridge or railway line or bridgehead from which the enemy may launch an attack otherwise impossible.

Mere Christianity

There is but one good; that is God. Everything else is good when it looks to Him and bad when it turns from Him. And the higher and mightier it is in the natural order, the more demoniac it will be if it rebels. It's not out of bad mice or bad fleas you make demons, but out of bad archangels. The false religion of lust is baser than the false religion of mother-love or patriotism or art: but lust is less likely to be made into a religion.

The Great Divorce

GRACE

If grace perfects nature it must expand all our natures into the full richness of the diversity which God intended when He made them, and Heaven will display far more variety than Hell.

Letters to Malcolm: Chiefly on Prayer

Sceptical, incredulous, materialistic ruts have been deeply engraved in our thought, perhaps even in our physical brains by all our earlier lives. At the slightest jerk our thought will flow down those old ruts. And notice when the jerks come. Usually at the precise moment when we might receive Grace. And if you were a devil would you not give the jerk just at those moments? I think that all Christians have found that he is v. active near the altar or on the eve of conversion: worldly anxieties, physical discomforts, lascivious fancies, doubt, are often poured in at such junctures . . . But the Grace is not frustrated. One gets more by pressing steadily on through these interruptions than on occasions when all goes smoothly . . .

I wouldn't now be bothered by a man who said to me "This, which you mistake for grace, is really the good functioning of your digestion." Does my digestion fall outside God's act? He made and allowed to me my colon as much as my guardian angel.

The Collected Letters of C. S. Lewis, Volume III

When God planted a garden He set a man over it and set the man under Himself. When He planted the garden of our nature and caused the flowering, fruiting loves to grow there, He set our will to "dress" them. Compared with them it is dry and cold. And unless His grace comes down, like the rain and the sunshine, we shall use this tool to little purpose. But its laborious—and largely negative—services are indispensable. If they were needed when the garden was still Paradisal, how much more now when the soil has gone sour and the worst weeds seem to thrive on it best? But heaven forbid we should work in the spirit of prigs and Stoics. While we hack and prune we know very well that what we are hacking and pruning is big with a splendour and vitality which our rational will could never of itself have supplied. To liberate that splendour, to let it become fully what it is trying to be, to have tall trees instead of scrubby tangles, and sweet apples instead of crabs, is part of our purpose.

The Four Loves

GRIEF

Real sorrow ends neither with a bang nor a whimper. Sometimes, after a spiritual journey like Dante's, down to the centre and then, terrace by terrace, up the mountain of accepted pain, it may rise into peace—but a peace hardly less severe than itself. Sometimes it remains for life, a puddle in the mind which grows always wider, shallower, and more unwholesome. Sometimes it just peters out, as other moods do. One of these alternatives has grandeur, but not tragic grandeur.

An Experiment in Criticism

Down here it is all loss and renunciation. The very purpose of the bereavement (so far as it affects ourselves) may have been to force this upon us. We are then compelled to try to believe, what we cannot yet feel, that God is our true Beloved. That is why bereavement is in some ways easier for the unbeliever than for us. He can storm and rage and shake his fist at the universe, and (if he is a genius) write poems like Houseman's or Hardy's. But we, at our lowest ebb, when the least effort seems too much for us, must begin to attempt what seem impossibilities.

The Four Loves

I have learned now that while those who speak about one's miseries usually hurt some, those who keep silence hurt more. They help to increase the sense of general isolation which makes a sort of fringe to the sorrow itself. You know what cogent reason I have to feel with you; but I can feel for you too. I know that what you are facing must be worse than what I must shortly face myself, because your happiness has lasted so much longer and is therefore so much more intertwined with your whole life. As Scott said in like case "What am I to do with that daily portion of my thoughts which has for so many years been hers?" People talk as if grief were just a feeling—as if it weren't the continually renewed shock of setting out again and again on familiar roads and being brought up short by the grim frontier post that now blocks them. I, to be sure, believe there is something beyond it; but the moment one tries to use that as a consolation (that is not its function) the belief crumbles. It is quite useless knocking at the door of heaven for earthly comfort; it's not the sort of comfort they supply there.

The Collected Letters of C. S. Lewis, Volume III

GUILT

It seems to me that the N.T., by preaching repentance and forgiveness, always assumes an audience who already believe in the Law of Nature and know they have disobeyed it. In modern England we cannot at present assume this, and therefore most apologetic begins a stage too far on. The first step is to create, or recover, the sense of guilt.

The Collected Letters of C. S. Lewis, Volume II

Remember the story in the *Imitation* [*The Imitation of Christ* by Thomas à Kempis], how the Christ on the crucifix suddenly spoke to the monk who was so anxious about his salvation and said "If you knew that all was well, what wd. you, to-day, do, or stop doing?" When you have found the answer, do it or stop doing it. You see, one must always get back to the practical and definite. What the devil loves is that vague cloud of unspecified guilt feeling or unspecified virtue by which he lures us into despair or presumption. "Details, please!" is the answer.

I wonder whether you are on the right track in expecting "stable sentiments" and "successful adjustment to life." This is the language of modern psychology rather than of religion or even of common experience, and I sometimes think that when the psychologists speak of adjustment to life they really mean perfect happiness and unbroken good fortune! Not to get—or, worse still, to be—what one wants is not a disease that can be cured, but the normal condition of man. To feel guilty, when one is guilty, and to realise, not without pain, one's moral and intellectual inadequacy is not a disease, but commonsense. To find that one's emotions do not "come to heel" and line up as stable sentiments in permanent conformity with one's convictions is simply the facts of being a fallen, and still imperfectly redeemed, man. We may be thankful if, by continual prayer and self-discipline, we can, over years, make some approach to that stability. After all, St. Paul, who was a good deal further along the road than you and I, could still write Romans, Chapter 7, verses 21–23.

The Collected Letters of C. S. Lewis, Volume III

HAPPINESS

What Satan put into the heads of our remote ancestors was the idea that they could "be like gods"—could set up on their own as if they had created themselves—be their own masters—invent some sort of happiness for themselves outside God, apart from God. And out of that hopeless attempt has come nearly all that we call human history—money, poverty, ambition, war, prostitution, classes, empires, slavery—the long terrible story of man trying to find something other than God which will make him happy.

God cannot give us a happiness and peace apart from Himself, because it is not there. There is no such thing.

Mere Christianity

There is a kind of happiness and wonder that makes you serious. It is too good to waste on jokes.

The Last Battle

When we are such as He can love without impediment, we shall in fact be happy.

The Problem of Pain

HEAVEN

But God will look to every soul like its first love because He is its first love. Your place in heaven will seem to be made for you and you alone, because you were made for it—made for it stitch by stitch as a glove is made for a hand.

The Problem of Pain

I am very surprised that your old anti-intellectualism should be so active—and yet perhaps I should not be since it is often said that conversion alters only the direction, not the character, of our minds. (This, by the bye, is very important and explains how personal and affectional relations between human souls can recognisably survive even in the full blaze of the beatific vision: and that if we are both saved I shall find you to all eternity in one sense still the same old Griffiths—indeed more the same than ever.)

The Collected Letters of C. S. Lewis, Volume II

Redeemed humanity is still young, it has hardly come to its full strength. But already there is joy enough in the little finger of a great saint such as yonder lady to waken all the dead things of the universe into life.

Everything becomes more and more itself. Here is joy that cannot be shaken. Our light can swallow up your darkness; but your darkness cannot now infect our light. No, no, no. Come to us. We will not go to you. Can you really have thought that love and joy would always be at the mercy of frowns and sighs? Did you not know they were stronger than their opposites?

The Great Divorce

The symbols under which Heaven is presented to us are (a) a dinner party, (b) a wedding, (c) a city, and (d) a concert. It would be grotesque to suppose that the guests or citizens or members of the choir didn't know one another. And how can love of one another be commanded in this life if it is to be cut short at death?

Think of yourself just as a seed patiently waiting in the earth: waiting to come up a flower in the Gardener's good time, up into the real world, the real waking. I suppose that our whole present life, looked back on from there, will seem only a drowsy half-waking. We are here in the land of dreams. But cock-crow is coming.

The Collected Letters of C. S. Lewis, Volume III

There is no morality in Heaven. The angels never knew (from within) the meaning of the word ought, and the blessed dead have long since gladly forgotten it. This is why Dante's Heaven is so right, and Milton's, with its military discipline, so silly.

Letters to Malcolm: Chiefly on Prayer

Tirian had thought—or he would have thought if he had time to think at all—that they were inside a little thatched stable, about twelve feet long and six feet wide. In reality they stood on grass, the deep blue sky was overhead, and the air which blew gently on their faces was that of a day in early summer. Not far away from them rose a grove of trees, thickly leaved, but under every leaf there peeped out the gold or faint yellow or purple or glowing red of fruits such as no one has seen in our world. The fruit made Tirian feel that it must be autumn but there was something in the feel of the air that told him it could not be later than June. They all moved towards the trees.

Everyone raised his hand to pick the fruit he best liked the look of, and then everyone paused for a second. This fruit was so beautiful that each felt "It can't be meant for me . . . surely we're not allowed to pluck it."

"It's all right," said Peter. "I know what we're all thinking. But I'm sure, quite sure, we needn't. I've a feeling we've got to the country where everything is allowed."

"Here goes, then!" said Eustace. And they all began to eat.

What was the fruit like? Unfortunately no one can describe a taste. All I can say is that, compared with those fruits, the freshest grapefruit you've ever eaten was dull, and the juiciest orange was dry, and the most melting pear was hard and woody, and the sweetest wild strawberry was sour. And there were no seeds or stones, and no wasps. If you had once eaten that fruit, all the nicest things in this world would taste like medicines after it. But I can't describe it. You can't find out what it is like unless you can get to that country and taste it for yourself.

The Last Battle

HELL

[The fictional George MacDonald is speaking.] "There are only two kinds of people in the end: those who say to God, 'Thy will be done' and those to whom God says, in the end, 'Thy will be done.' All that are in Hell choose it. Without that self-choice, there could be no Hell. No soul that seriously and constantly desires joy will ever miss it. Those who seek, find. To those who knock, it is opened.". . .

"Hell is a state of mind—ye never said a truer word. And every state of mind, left to itself, every shutting up of the creature within the dungeon of its own mind is, in the end, Hell. But Heaven is not a state of mind. Heaven is reality itself. All that is fully real is Heavenly.". . .

"Hell is smaller than one pebble of your earthly world: but it is smaller than one atom of this world, the Real World. Look at yon butterfly. If it swallowed all Hell, Hell would not be big enough to do it any harm or to have any taste. . . .

"A damned soul is nearly nothing: it is shrunk, shut up in itself. Good beats upon the damned incessantly as sound waves beat on the ears of the deaf, but they cannot receive it. Their fists are clenched, their teeth are clenched, their eyes fast shut. First they will not, in the end they cannot, open their hands for gifts, or their mouths for food, or their eyes to see."

"Then no one can ever reach them?"

"Only the Greatest of all can make Himself small enough to enter Hell. For the higher a thing is, the lower it can descend—a man can sympathise with a horse but a horse cannot sympathise with a rat. Only One has descended into Hell."

The Great Divorce

A black hole is blackness enclosed, limited. And in that sense the Landlord has made the black hole. He has put into the world a Worst Thing. But evil of itself would never reach a worst: for evil is fissiparous and could never in a thousand eternities find any way to arrest its own reproduction. If it could, it would be no longer evil: for Form and Limit belong to the good. The walls of the black hole are the tourniquet on the wound through which the lost soul else would bleed to a death she never reached. It is the Landlord's last service to those who will let Him do nothing better for them.

The Pilgrim's Regress

It's not a question of God "sending" us to Hell. In each of us there is something growing up which will of itself *be Hell* unless it is nipped in the bud.

God in the Dock

There is no doctrine which I would more willingly remove from Christianity than this, if it lay in my power. But it has the full support of Scripture and, specially, of Our Lord's own words; it has always been held by Christendom; and it has the support of reason. If a game is played, it must be possible to lose it. If the happiness of a creature lies in self-surrender, no one can make that surrender but himself (though many can help him to make it) and he may refuse. I would pay any price to be able to say truthfully "All will be saved." But my reason retorts, "Without their will, or with it?" If I say "Without their will" I at once perceive a contradiction; how can the supreme voluntary act of self-surrender be involuntary? If I say "With their will," my reason replies "How if they will not give in?". . .

The doors of Hell are locked on the inside. I do not mean that the ghosts may not wish to come out of Hell, in the vague fashion wherein an envious man "wishes" to be happy: but they certainly do not will even the first preliminary stages of that self-abandonment through which alone the soul can reach any good. They enjoy forever the horrible freedom they have demanded, and are therefore self-enslaved: just as the blessed, forever submitting to obedience, become through all eternity more and more free.

The Problem of Pain

"I am troubled, Sir," said I, "because that unhappy creature doesn't seem to me to be the sort of soul that ought to be even in danger of damnation. She isn't wicked: she's only a silly, garrulous old woman who has got into a habit of grumbling, and one feels that a little kindness, and rest, and change would put her all right."

"That is what she once was. That is maybe what she still is. If so, she certainly will be cured. But the whole question is whether she is now a grumbler."

"I should have thought there was no doubt about that!"

"Aye, but ye misunderstand me. The question is whether she is a grumbler, or only a grumble. If there is a real woman—even the least trace of one—still there inside the grumbling, it can be brought to life again. If there's one wee spark under all those ashes, we'll blow it till the whole pile is red and clear. But if there's nothing but ashes we'll not go on blowing them in our own eyes forever. They must be swept up."

"But how can there be a grumble without a grumbler?"

"The whole difficulty of understanding Hell is that the thing to be understood is so nearly Nothing. But ye'll have had experiences . . . It begins with a grumbling mood, and yourself still distinct from it: perhaps criticising it. And yourself, in a dark hour, may will that mood, embrace it. Ye can repent and come out of it again. But there may come a day when you can do that no longer. Then there will be no you left to criticise the mood, nor even to enjoy it, but just the grumble itself going on forever like a machine."

The Great Divorce

HOLINESS

How little people know who think that holiness is dull. When one meets the real thing . . . it is irresistible. If even 10 percent of the world's population had it, would not the whole world be converted and happy before a year's end?

The Collected Letters of C. S. Lewis, Volume III

If He does not support us, not one of us is safe from some gross sin. On the other hand, no possible degree of holiness or heroism which has ever been recorded of the greatest saints is beyond what He is determined to produce in every one of us in the end. The job will not be completed in this life: but He means to get us as far as possible before death.

Mere Christianity

HOLY SPIRIT

It is as if a sort of communal personality came into existence. Of course, it is not a real person: it is only rather like a person. But that is just one of the differences between God and us. What grows out of the joint life of the Father and Son is a real Person, is in fact the Third of the three Persons who are God.

This third Person is called, in technical language, the Holy Ghost or the "spirit" of God. Do not be worried or surprised if you find it (or Him) rather vaguer or more shadowy in your mind than the other two. I think there is a reason why that must be so. In the Christian life you are not usually looking at Him: He is always acting through you. If you think of the Father as something "out there," in front of you, and of the Son as someone standing at your side, helping you to pray, trying to turn you into another son, then you have to think of the third Person as something inside you, or behind you. Perhaps some people might find it easier to begin with the third Person and work backwards. God is love, and that love works through men—especially through the whole community of Christians. But this spirit of love is, from all eternity, a love going on between the Father and Son.

Mere Christianity

I don't doubt that the Holy Spirit guides your decisions from within when you make them with the intention of pleasing God. The error wd. be to think that He speaks only within, whereas in reality He speaks also through Scripture, the Church, Christian friends, books, etc.

The Collected Letters of C. S. Lewis, Volume III

If the Holy Spirit speaks in the man, then in prayer God speaks to God. But the human petitioner does not therefore become a "dream." As you said the other day, God and man cannot exclude one another, as man excludes man, at the point of junction, so to call it, between Creator and creature; the point where the mystery of creation—timeless for God, and incessant in time for us—is actually taking place. "God did (or said) it" and "I did (or said) it" can both be true.

Letters to Malcolm: Chiefly on Prayer

Lucy looked along the beam and presently saw something in it. At first it looked like a cross, then it looked like an aeroplane, then it looked like a kite, and at last with a whirring of wings it was right overhead and was an albatross. It circled three times round the mast and then perched for an instant on the crest of the gilded dragon at the prow. It called out in a strong sweet voice what seemed to be words though no one understood them. After that it spread its wings, rose, and began to fly slowly ahead, bearing a little to starboard. Drinian steered after it not doubting that it offered good guidance. But no one except Lucy knew that as it circled the mast it had whispered to her, "Courage, dear heart," and the voice, she felt sure, was Aslan's, and with the voice a delicious smell breathed in her face.

The Voyage of the DAWN TREADER

It is quite right that you should feel that "something terrific" has happened to you (It has) and be "all glowy." Accept these sensations with thankfulness as birthday cards from God, but remember that they are only greetings, not the real gift. I mean, it is not the sensations that are the real thing. The real thing is the gift of the Holy Spirit which can't usually be—perhaps not ever—experienced as a sensation or emotion. The sensations are merely the response of your nervous system. Don't depend on them. Otherwise when they go and you are once more emotionally flat (as you certainly will be quite soon), you might think that the real thing had gone too. But it won't. It will be there when you can't feel it. May even be most operative when you can feel it least.

The Collected Letters of C. S. Lewis, Volume III

HOPE

Hope is one of the Theological virtues. This means that a continual looking forward to the eternal world is not (as some modern people think) a form of escapism or wishful thinking, but one of the things a Christian is meant to do. It does not mean that we are to leave the present world as it is. If you read history you will find that the Christians who did most for the present world were just those who thought most of the next. The Apostles themselves, who set on foot the conversion of the Roman Empire, the great men who built up the Middle Ages, the English Evangelicals who abolished the Slave Trade, all left their mark on Earth, precisely because their minds were occupied with Heaven. It is since Christians have largely ceased to think of the other world that they have become so ineffective in this. Aim at Heaven and you will get earth "thrown in": aim at earth and you will get neither. . . .

The Christian says, "Creatures are not born with desires unless satisfaction for those desires exists. A baby feels hunger: well, there is such a thing as food. A duckling wants to swim: well, there is such a thing as water. Men feel sexual desire: well, there is such a thing as sex. If I find in myself a desire which no experience in this world can satisfy, the most probable explanation is that I was made for another world. If none of my earthly pleasures satisfy it, that does not prove that the universe is a fraud. Probably earthly pleasures were never meant to satisfy it, but only to arouse it, to suggest the real thing. If that is so, I must take care, on the one hand, never to despise, or be unthankful for, these earthly blessings, and on the other, never to mistake them for the something else of which they are only a kind of copy, or echo, or mirage. I must keep alive in myself the desire for my true country, which I shall not find till after death; I must never let it get snowed under or turned aside; I must make it the main object of life to press on to that other country and to help others to do the same."

There is no need to be worried by facetious people who try to make the Christian hope of "Heaven" ridiculous by saying they do not want "to spend eternity playing harps." The answer to such people is that if they cannot understand books written for grown-ups, they should not talk about them. All the scriptural imagery (harps, crowns, gold, etc.) is, of course, a merely symbolical attempt to express the inexpressible. Musical instruments are mentioned because for many people (not all) music is the thing known in the present life which most strongly suggests ecstasy and infinity. Crowns are mentioned to suggest the fact that those who are united with God in eternity share His splendour and power and joy. Gold is mentioned to suggest the timelessness of Heaven (gold does not rust) and the preciousness of it. People who take these symbols literally might as well think that when Christ told us to be like doves, He meant that we were to lay eggs.

Mere Christianity

Then Aslan turned to them and said:

"You do not yet look so happy as I mean you to be."

Lucy said, "We're so afraid of being sent away, Aslan. And you have sent us back into our own world so often."

"No fear of that," said Aslan. "Have you not guessed?"

Their hearts leaped and a wild hope rose within them.

"There was a real railway accident," said Aslan softly.

"Your father and mother and all of you are—as you used to call it in the Shadowlands—dead. The term is over: the holidays have begun. The dream is ended: this is the morning."

And as He spoke He no longer looked to them like a lion; but the things that began to happen after that were so great and beautiful that I cannot write them. And for us this is the end of all the stories, and we can most truly say that they all lived happily ever after. But for them it was only the beginning of the real story. All their life in this world and all their adventures in Narnia had only been the cover and the title page: now at last they were beginning Chapter One of the Great Story which no one on earth has read: which goes on forever: in which every chapter is better than the one before.

The Last Battle

HUMANITY

"You come of the Lord Adam and the Lady Eve," said Aslan. "And that is both honour enough to erect the head of the poorest beggar, and shame enough to bow the shoulders of the greatest emperor in earth. Be content."

Prince Caspian

We must not listen to Pope's maxim about the proper study of mankind. The proper study of man is everything. The proper study of man as artist is everything which gives a foothold to the imagination and the passions.

C. S. Lewis on Stories

ON BEING HUMAN

Angelic minds, they say, by simple intelligence
Behold the Forms of nature. They discern
Unerringly the Archetypes, all the verities
Which mortals lack or indirectly learn.
Transparent in primordial truth, unvarying,
Pure Earthness and right Stonehood from their clear,
High eminence are seen; unveiled, the seminal
Huge Principles appear.

The Tree-ness of the tree they know—the meaning of
Arboreal life, how from earth's salty lap
The solar beam uplifts it, all the holiness
Enacted by leaves' fall and rising sap;
But never an angel knows the knife-edged severance
Of sun from shadow where the trees begin,
The blessed cool at every pore caressing us
—An angel has no skin.

They see the Form of Air; but mortals breathing it
Drink the whole summer down into the breast.
The lavish pinks, the field new-mown, the ravishing
Sea-smells, the wood-fire smoke that whispers Rest.
The tremor on the rippled pool of memory
That from each smell in widening circles goes,
The pleasure and the pang—can angels measure it?
An angel has no nose.

The nourishing of life, and how it flourishes
On death, and why, they utterly know; but not
The hill-born, earthy spring, the dark cold bilberries,
The ripe peach from the southern wall still hot,
Full-bellied tankards foamy-topped, the delicate
Half-lyric lamb, a new loaf's billowy curves,
Nor porridge, nor the tingling taste of oranges—
An angel has no nerves.

Far richer they! I know the senses' witchery
Guards us, like air, from heavens too big to see;
Imminent death to man that barb'd sublimity
And dazzling edge of beauty unsheathed would be.
Yet here, within this tiny, charm'd interior,
This parlour of the brain, their Maker shares
With living men some secrets in a privacy
Forever ours, not theirs.

The Collected Poems of C. S. Lewis

HUMILITY

And that is enough to raise our thoughts to what may happen when the redeemed soul, beyond all hope and nearly beyond belief, learns at last that she has pleased Him whom she was created to please. There will be no room for vanity then. She will be free from the miserable illusion that it is her doing. With no taint of what we should now call self-approval she will most innocently rejoice in the thing that God has made her to be, and the moment which heals her old inferiority complex for ever will also drown her pride deeper than Prospero's book. Perfect humility dispenses with modesty. If God is satisfied with the work, the work may be satisfied with itself: "it is not for her to bandy compliments with her Sovereign."

The Weight of Glory

Do not imagine that if you meet a really humble man he will be what most people call "humble" nowadays: he will not be a sort of greasy, smarmy person, who is always telling you that, of course, he is nobody. Probably all you will think about him is that he seemed a cheerful, intelligent chap who took a real interest in what you said to him. If you do dislike him it will be because you feel a little envious of anyone who seems to enjoy life so easily. He will not be thinking about humility: he will not be thinking about himself at all.

If anyone would like to acquire humility, I can, I think, tell him the first step. The first step is to realise that one is proud. And a biggish step, too. At least, nothing whatever can be done before it. If you think you are not conceited, it means you are very conceited indeed.

Mere Christianity

For each of us the Baptist's words are true: "He must increase and I decrease." He will be infinitely merciful to our repeated failures; I know no promise that He will accept a deliberate compromise. For He has, in the last resort, nothing to give us but Himself; and He can give that only in so far as our self-affirming will retires and makes room for Him in our souls.

The Weight of Glory

IMMORTALITY

I think that Resurrection (what ever it exactly means) is so much profounder an idea than mere immortality. I am sure we don't just "go on." We really die and are really built up again.

The Collected Letters of C. S. Lewis, Volume II

Thanks for your kind letter. I believe in the resurrection, and also (rather less confidently) in the natural immortality of the soul. But the state of the dead till the resurrection is unimaginable. Are they in the same time that we live in at all? And if not, is there any sense in asking what they are "now"?

The Collected Letters of C. S. Lewis, Volume III

Immortality makes this other difference, which, by the by, has a connection with the difference between totalitarianism and democracy. If individuals live only seventy years, then a state, or a nation, or a civilisation, which may last for a thousand years, is more important than an individual. But if Christianity is true, then the individual is not only more important but incomparably more important, for he is everlasting and the life of a state or a civilisation, compared with his, is only a moment.

Mere Christianity

Resurrection was not regarded simply or chiefly as evidence for the immortality of the soul. It is, of course, often so regarded to-day: I have heard a man maintain that "the importance of the

Resurrection is that it proves survival." Such a view cannot at any point be reconciled with the language of the New Testament. On such a view Christ would simply have done what all men do when they die: the only novelty would have been that in His case we were allowed to see it happening. But there is not in Scripture the faintest suggestion that the Resurrection was new evidence for something that had in fact been always happening.

Miracles

I can (quite often) believe in my own death and in that of the species, for I have seen that kind of thing happening. I can believe with nerves and imagination as well as intellect, in human immortality; when it comes it will be no more astonishing than certain other wakenings that I have experienced. To live by hope and longing is an art that was taught at my school. It does not surprise me that there should be two worlds.

Present Concerns

INCARNATION

The Second Person in God, the Son, became human Himself: was born into the world as an actual man—a real man of a particular height, with hair of a particular colour, speaking a particular language, weighing so many stone. The Eternal Being, who knows everything and who created the whole universe, became not only a man but (before that) a baby, and before that a foetus inside a Woman's body. If you want to get the hang of it, think how you would like to become a slug or a crab.

Mere Christianity

The story [of the Incarnation] is strangely like many myths which have haunted religion from the first, and yet it is not like them. It is not transparent to the reason: we could not have invented it ourselves. It has not the suspicious a priori lucidity of Pantheism or of Newtonian physics. It has the seemingly arbitrary and idiosyncratic character which modern science is slowly teaching us to put up with in this wilful universe, where energy is made up in little parcels of a quantity no one could predict, where speed is not unlimited, where irreversible entropy gives time a real direction and the cosmos, no longer static or cyclic, moves like a drama from a real beginning to a real end. If any message from the core of reality ever were to reach us, we should expect to find in it just that unexpectedness, that wilful, dramatic anfractuosity which we find in the Christian faith. It has the master touch—the rough, male taste of reality, not made by us, or, indeed, for us, but hitting us in the face.

The Problem of Pain

One must be careful not to put this in a way which would blur the distinction between the creation of a man and the Incarnation of God. Could one, as a mere model, put it thus? In creation God makes—invents—a person and "utters"—injects—him into the realm of Nature. In the Incarnation, God the Son takes the body and human soul of Jesus, and, through that, the whole environment of Nature, all the creaturely predicament, into His own being. So that "He came down from Heaven" can almost be transposed into "Heaven drew earth up into it," and locality, limitation, sleep, sweat, footsore weariness, frustration, pain, doubt, and death, are, from before all worlds, known by God from within. The pure light walks the earth; the darkness, received into the heart of Deity, is there swallowed up. Where, except in uncreated light, can the darkness be drowned?

Letters to Malcolm: Chiefly on Prayer

INTERRUPTIONS

Have you had glorious fogs—frost-fogs? We have had some of the finest I have ever seen. In fact we have had all sorts of beauty—outside. Inside myself the situation seems quite the reverse. I seem to go steadily downhill and backwards. I am certainly further from self-control and charity and light than I was last spring. Now that W. is with us I don't get enough solitude: or so I say to myself in excuse, knowing all the time that what God demands is our solution of the problem set, not of some other problem which we think He ought to have set: and that what we call hindrances are really the raw material of spiritual life. As if the fire should call the coal a hindrance! (One can imagine a little young fire, which had been getting along nicely with the sticks and paper, regarding it as a mere cruelty when the big lumps were put on: never dreaming what a huge steady glow, how far surpassing its present crackling infancy, the Tender of the Fire designed when He stoked it.)

The Collected Letters of C. S. Lewis, Volume I

The great thing, if one can, is to stop regarding all the unpleasant things as interruptions of one's "own" or "real" life. The truth is of course that what one calls the interruptions are precisely one's real life—the life God is sending one day by day: what one calls one's "real life" is a phantom of one's own imagination.

The Collected Letters of C. S. Lewis, Volume II

My own experience in reading the Gospels was at one stage even more depressing than yours. Everyone told me that there I should find a figure whom I couldn't help loving. Well, I could. They told me I would final moral perfection—but one sees so very little of Him in ordinary situations that I couldn't make much of that either. Indeed some of His behaviour seemed to me open to criticism, e.g., accepting an invitation to dine with a Pharisee and then loading him with torrents of abuse.

Now the truth is, I think, that the sweetly-attractive-human-Jesus is a product of 19th century scepticism, produced by people who were ceasing to believe in His divinity but wanted to keep as much Christianity as they could. It is not what an unbeliever coming to the records with an open mind will (at first) find there. The first thing you find is that we are simply not invited to speak, to pass any moral judgement on Him, however favourable: it is only too clear that He is going to do whatever judging there is: it is we who are being judged, sometimes tenderly, sometimes with stunning severity, but always *de haut en bas* ["from top to bottom"]. (Have you ever noticed that your imagination can hardly be forced to picture Him as shorter than yourself?)

The first real work of the Gospels on a fresh reader is, and ought to be, to raise very acutely the question, "Who or What is this?" For there is a good deal in the character which, unless He really is what He says He is, is not lovable or even tolerable. If He is, then of course it is another matter: nor will it then be surprising if much remains puzzling to the end. For if there is anything in Christianity, we are now approaching something which will never be fully comprehensible.

The Collected Letters of C. S. Lewis, Volume II

What are we to make of Jesus Christ? This question which has, in a sense, a frantically comic side. For the real question is not what are we to make of Christ, but what is He to make of us? The picture of a fly sitting deciding what it is going to make of an elephant has comic elements about it. But perhaps the questioner meant what are we to make of Him in the sense of "How are we to solve the historical problem set us by the recorded sayings and acts of this Man?" This problem is to reconcile two things. On the one hand you have got the almost generally admitted depth and sanity of His moral teaching, which is not very seriously questioned, even by those who are opposed to Christianity. . . .

The other phenomenon is the quite appalling nature of this Man's theological remarks. You all know what I mean, and I want rather to stress the point that the appalling claim which this Man seems to be making is not merely made at one moment of His career. There is, of course, the one moment which led to His execution. The moment at which the High Priest said to Him, "Who are you?" "I am the Anointed, the Son of the uncreated God, and you shall see Me appearing at the end of all history as the judge of the Universe.". . .

On the one side clear, definite moral teaching. On the other, claims which, if not true, are those of a megalomaniac, compared with whom Hitler was the most sane and humble of men. There is no half-way house and there is no parallel in other religions. If you had gone to Buddha and asked him "Are you the son of Bramah?" he would have said, "My son, you are still in the vale of illusion." If you had gone to Socrates and asked, "Are you Zeus?" he would have laughed at you. If you had gone to Mohammed and asked, "Are you Allah?" he would first have rent his clothes and then cut your head off. If you had asked Confucius, "Are you Heaven?" I think he would have probably replied, "Remarks which are not in accordance with nature are in bad taste." The idea of a great moral teacher saying what Christ said is out of the question. In my opinion, the only person who can say that sort of thing is either God or a complete lunatic suffering from that form of delusion which undermines the whole mind of man. If you think you are a poached egg, when you are looking for a piece of toast to suit you, you may be sane, but if you think you are God, there is no chance for you. . . .

The things He says are very different from what any other teacher has said. Others say, "This is the truth about the Universe. This is the way you ought to go," but He says, "I am the Truth, and the Way, and the Life." He says, "No man can reach absolute reality, except through Me. Try to retain your own life and you will be inevitably ruined. Give yourself away and you will be saved." He says, "If you are ashamed of Me, if, when you hear this call, you turn the other way, I also will look the other way when I come again as God without disguise. If anything whatever is keeping you from God and from Me, whatever it is, throw it away. If it is your eye, pull it out. If it is your hand, cut it off. If you put yourself first you will be last. Come to Me everyone who is carrying a heavy load, I will set that right. Your sins, all of them, are wiped out, I can do that. I am Re-birth, I am Life. Eat Me, drink Me, I am your Food. And finally, do not be afraid, I have overcome the whole Universe." That is the issue.

God in the Dock

Yes, Jesus Himself, of course: the heart. Not only the God in Him but the historical Man. I don't know that I ever got much from reading things about Him. Perhaps, in a queer way, I got most from reading the Apocryphal Gospels (the whole Apocryphal N.T. is done in one vol. ed. M. R. James). For there you find things attributed to Him that couldn't be true. You even find wise & beautiful sayings which nevertheless just don't ring true. And have you noticed—reading the true sayings in the real Gospels—how hardly one of them cd. have been guessed in advance?

The Collected Letters of C. S. Lewis, Volume III

JOY

I want to stress what I think that we (or at least I) need more;
the joy and delight in God which meet us in the Psalms, however
loosely or closely, in this or that instance, they may be connected
with the Temple. This is the living centre of Judaism. These poets
knew far less reason than we for loving God. They did not know
that He offered them eternal joy; still less that He would die to
win it for them. Yet they express a longing for Him, for His mere
presence, which comes only to the best Christians or to Christians in their best moments. They long to live all their days in
the Temple so that they may constantly see "the fair beauty of
the Lord" ([Ps.]27, 4). Their longing to go up to Jerusalem and
"appear before the presence of God" is like a physical thirst (42).
From Jerusalem His presence flashes out "in perfect beauty" (50,
2). Lacking that encounter with Him, their souls are parched like
a waterless countryside (63, 2). They crave to be "satisfied with
the pleasures" of His house (65, 4). Only there can they be at
ease, like a bird in the nest (84, 3). One day of those "pleasures"
is better than a lifetime spent elsewhere (10).

Reflections on the Psalms

In a sense, the central story of my life is about nothing else. . . . It
is that of an unsatisfied desire which is itself more desirable than
any other satisfaction. I call it Joy, which is here a technical term
and must be sharply distinguished both from Happiness and from
Pleasure. Joy (in my sense) has indeed one characteristic, and one

179

only, in common with them: the fact that anyone who has experienced it will want it again. Apart from that and considered only in its quality, it might almost equally be called unhappiness or grief. But then it is a kind we want. I doubt whether anyone who has tasted it would ever, if both were in his power, exchange it for all the pleasures in the world. But then, joy is never in our power and pleasure often is.

Surprised by Joy

Joy is the serious business of Heaven.

Letters to Malcolm: Chiefly on Prayer

In speaking of this desire for our own far-off country, which we find in ourselves even now, I feel a certain shyness. I am almost committing an indecency. I am trying to rip open the inconsolable secret in each one of you—the secret which hurts so much that you take your revenge on it by calling it names like Nostalgia and Romanticism and Adolescence: the secret also which pierces with such sweetness that when, in very intimate conversation, the mention of it becomes imminent, we grow awkward and affect to laugh at ourselves: the secret we cannot hide and cannot tell, though we desire to do both. We cannot tell it because it is a desire for something that has never actually appeared in our experience. We cannot hide it because our experience is constantly suggesting it, and we betray ourselves like lovers at the mention of a name. Our commonest expedient is to call it beauty and behave as if that had settled the matter. Wordsworth's expedient was to identify it with certain moments in his own past. But all this is a cheat. If Wordsworth had gone back to those moments in the past, he would not have found the thing itself, but only the reminder of it; what he remembered would turn out to be itself a remembering. The books or the music in which we thought the beauty was located will betray us if we trust to them; it was not in them, it only came through them, and what came through them was longing. These things—the beauty, the memory of our own past—are good images of what we really desire; but if they are mistaken for the thing itself they turn into dumb idols, breaking the hearts of their worshippers. For they are not the thing itself; they are only the scent of a flower we have not found, the echo of a tune we have not heard, news from a country we have never yet visited. . . .

Apparently, then, our lifelong nostalgia, our longing to be re-united with something in the universe from which we now feel cut off, to be on the inside of some door which we have always seen from the outside, is no mere neurotic fancy, but the truest index of our real situation. And to be at last summoned inside would be both glory and honour beyond all our merits and also the healing of that old ache. . . . The whole man is to drink joy from the fountain of joy.

The Weight of Glory

KINDNESS

Love is something more stern and splendid than mere kindness.

For about a hundred years we have so concentrated on one of the virtues—"kindness" or mercy—that most of us do not feel anything except kindness to be really good or anything but cruelty to be really bad. Such lopsided ethical developments are not uncommon, and other ages too have had their pet virtues and curious insensibilities. And if one virtue must be cultivated at the expense of all the rest, none has a higher claim than mercy.... The real trouble is that "kindness" is a quality fatally easy to attribute to ourselves on quite inadequate grounds. Everyone feels benevolent if nothing happens to be annoying him at the moment. Thus a man easily comes to console himself for all his other vices by a conviction that "his heart's in the right place" and "he wouldn't hurt a fly," though in fact he has never made the slightest sacrifice for a fellow creature. We think we are kind when we are only happy: it is not so easy, on the same grounds, to imagine oneself temperate, chaste, or humble.

You cannot be kind unless you have all the other virtues. If, being cowardly, conceited and slothful, you have never yet done a fellow creature great mischief, that is only because your neighbour's welfare has not yet happened to conflict with your safety, self-approval, or ease. Every vice leads to cruelty.

The Problem of Pain

But, in reality, along with the power to forgive, we have lost the power to condemn. If a taste for cruelty and a taste for kindness were equally ultimate and basic, by what common standard could the one reprove the other? In reality, cruelty does not come from desiring evil as such, but from perverted sexuality, inordinate resentment, or lawless ambition and avarice.

God in the Dock

Now the very Pagans knew that any beggar at your door might be a god in disguise: and the parable of the sheep and the goats is Our Lord's comment. What you do, or don't do, to the beggar, you do, or don't do, to Him. Taken at the Pantheist extreme, this could mean that men are only appearances of God—dramatic representations, as it were. Taken at the Legalist extreme, it could mean that God, by a sort of Legal fiction, will "deem" your kindness to the beggar a kindness done to Himself. Or again, as Our Lord's own words suggest, that since the least of men are His "brethren," the whole action is, so to speak, "within the family." And in what sense brethren? Biologically, because Jesus is Man? Ontologically, because the light lightens them all? Or simply "loved like brethren." (It cannot refer only to the regenerate.) I would ask first whether any one of these formulations is "right" in a sense which makes the others simply wrong?

Letters to Malcolm: Chiefly on Prayer

KNOWING GOD

"Son," said Aslan to the Cabby. "I have known you long. Do you know me?"

"Well, no sir," said the Cabby. "Leastways, not in an ordinary manner of speaking. Yet I feel somehow, if I may make so free, as 'ow we've met before."

"It is well," said the Lion. "You know better than you think you know, and you shall live to know me better yet."

The Magician's Nephew

"But who is Aslan? Do you know him?"

"Well—he knows me," said Edmund. "He is the great Lion, the son of the Emperor over Sea, who saved me and saved Narnia."

The Voyage of the DAWN TREADER

The naif image is mischievous chiefly in so far as it holds unbelievers back from conversion. It does believers, even at its crudest, no harm. What soul ever perished for believing that God the Father really has a beard?

Letters to Malcolm: Chiefly on Prayer

FOOTNOTE TO ALL PRAYERS

He whom I bow to only knows to whom I bow
When I attempt the ineffable name, murmuring Thou;
And dream of Pheidian fancies and embrace in heart

Meanings, I know, that cannot be the thing thou art.
All prayers always, taken at their word, blaspheme,
Invoking with frail imageries a folklore dream;
And all men are idolaters, crying unheard
To senseless idols, if thou take them at their word,
And all men in their praying, self-deceived, address
One that is not (so saith that old rebuke) unless
Thou, of mere grace, appropriate, and to thee divert
Men's arrows, all at hazard aimed, beyond desert.
Take not, oh Lord, our literal sense, but in thy great,
Unbroken speech our halting metaphor translate.

The Pilgrim's Regress, The Collected Poems of C. S. Lewis

Every idea of Him we form, He must in mercy shatter. The most blessed result of prayer would be to rise thinking "But I never knew before. I never dreamed . . ." I suppose it was at such a moment that Thomas Aquinas said of all his own theology, "It reminds me of straw."

Letters to Malcolm: Chiefly on Prayer

LIFE

The glory of God, and, as our only means to glorifying Him, the salvation of human souls, is the real business of life.

Christian Reflections

Have you found, or is it peculiar to me, that it is much easier to pray for others than for oneself? Doubtless because every return to one's own situation involves action: or to speak more plainly, obedience. That appears to me more and more the whole business of life, the only road to love and peace—the cross and the crown in one.

The Collected Letters of C. S. Lewis, Volume II

"When that which is perfect is come, then that which is in part shall be done away" [I Cor. 13:10]. The idea of reaching "a good life" without Christ is based on a double error. Firstly, we cannot do it; and secondly, in setting up "a good life" as our final goal, we have missed the very point of our existence. Morality is a mountain which we cannot climb by our own efforts; and if we could we should only perish in the ice and unbreathable air of the summit, lacking those wings with which the rest of the journey has to be accomplished. For it is from there that the real ascent begins. The ropes and axes are "done away" and the rest is a matter of flying.

God in the Dock

LIFE AFTER DEATH

My friendship [with Charles Williams] is not ended. His death has had the very unexpected effect of making death itself look quite different. I believe in the next life ten times more strongly than I did. At moments it seems almost tangible. Mr. Dyson, on the day of the funeral, summed up what many of us felt. "It is not blasphemous," he said. "To believe that what was true of Our Lord is, in its less degree, true of all who are in Him. They go away in order to be with us in a new way, even closer than before." A month ago I wd. have called this silly sentiment. Now I know better. He seems, in some indefinable way, to be all around us now. I do not doubt he is doing and will do for us all sorts of things he could not have done while in the body.

The Collected Letters of C. S. Lewis, Volume II

Note that life after death, which still seems to you the essential thing, was itself a late revelation. God trained the Hebrews for centuries to believe in Him without promising them an after-life: and, blessings on Him, He trained me in the same way for about a year. It is like the disguised prince in a fairy tale who wins the heroine's love before she knows he is anything more than a wood-cutter. What wd. be a bribe if it came first had better come last.

I wasn't at all questioning the life after death, you know: only saying that its character is for us unimaginable. The things you tell me about it are all outside my knowledge and most of them outside my powers of conception. To say "They are now as they were then" and add next moment "unhampered of course by the body" is to me like saying "They are exactly the same but of course unimaginably different."

But don't let us trouble one another about it. We shall know when we are dead ourselves. The Bible seems scrupulously to avoid any descriptions of the other world, or worlds, except in terms of parable or allegory.

The Collected Letters of C. S. Lewis, Volume III

LONGING

It appeared to me therefore that if a man diligently followed this desire, pursuing the false objects until their falsity appeared and then resolutely abandoning them, he must come out at last into the clear knowledge that the human soul was made to enjoy some object that is never fully given—nay, cannot even be imagined as given—in our present mode of subjective and spatio-temporal experience. This Desire was, in the soul, as the Siege Perilous in Arthur's castle—the chair in which only one could sit. And if nature makes nothing in vain, the One who can sit in this chair must exist. I knew only too well how easily the longing accepts false objects and through what dark ways the pursuit of them leads us: but I also saw that the Desire itself contains the corrective of all these errors. The only fatal error was to pretend that you had passed from desire to fruition, when, in reality, you had found either nothing, or desire itself, or the satisfaction of some different desire.

The Pilgrim's Regress

Joy is distinct not only from pleasure in general but even from aesthetic pleasure. It must have the stab, the pang, the inconsolable longing. . . .

All Joy reminds. It is never a possession, always a desire for something longer ago or further away or still "about to be."

Surprised by Joy

All joy (as distinct from mere pleasure, still more amusement) emphasises our pilgrim status; always reminds, beckons, awakens desire. Our best havings are wantings.

The Collected Letters of C. S. Lewis, Volume III

LORD'S PRAYER

For many years after my conversion I never used any ready-made forms except the Lord's Prayer.

Letters to Malcolm: Chiefly on Prayer

If you are interested enough to have read thus far you are probably interested enough to make a shot at saying your prayers: and, whatever else you say, you will probably say the Lord's Prayer.

Its very first words are Our Father. Do you now see what those words mean? They mean quite frankly, that you are putting yourself in the place of a son of God. To put it bluntly, you are dressing up as Christ. If you like, you are pretending. Because, of course, the moment you realise what the words mean, you realise that you are not a son of God. You are not being like The Son of God, whose will and interests are at one with those of the Father: you are a bundle of self-centred fears, hopes, greeds, jealousies, and self-conceit, all doomed to death. So that, in a way, this dressing up as Christ is a piece of outrageous cheek. But the odd thing is that He has ordered us to do it.

Mere Christianity

A nobler analogy, sanctioned by the constant tenor of Our Lord's teaching, is that between God's love for man and a father's love for a son. Whenever this is used, however (that is, whenever we pray the Lord's Prayer), it must be remembered that the Saviour used it in a time and place where paternal authority stood much higher than it does in modern England. A father half apologetic for having brought his son into the world, afraid to restrain him lest he should create inhibitions or even to instruct him lest he should interfere with his independence of mind, is a most misleading symbol of the Divine Fatherhood.

The Problem of Pain

"Thy will be done." But a great deal of it is to be done by God's creatures; including me. The petition, then, is not merely that I may patiently suffer God's will but also that I may vigorously do it. I must be an agent as well as a patient.

Letters to Malcolm: Chiefly on Prayer

I do not mean that the words "Thy will be done" are merely a submission. They should, and if we make progress they will increasingly, be the voice of joyful desire, free of hunger and thirst, and I argue very heartily that to treat them simply as a clause of submission or renunciation greatly impoverishes the prayer.

Christian Reflections

"Give us our daily bread" (not an annuity for life) applies to spiritual gifts too: the little daily support for the daily trial. Life has to be taken day by day & hour by hour.

The Collected Letters of C. S. Lewis, Volume III

We believe that God forgives us our sins; but also that He will not do so unless we forgive other people their sins against us. There is no doubt about the second part of this statement. It is in the Lord's Prayer; it was emphatically stated by our Lord. If you don't forgive, you will not be forgiven. No part of His teaching is clearer, and there are no exceptions to it. He doesn't say that we are to forgive other people's sins provided they are not too frightful, or provided there are extenuating circumstances, or anything of that sort. We are to forgive them all, however spiteful, however mean, however often they are repeated. If we don't, we shall be forgiven none of our own.

The Weight of Glory

Our Father,
    I join with all the angels and the saints in hallowing Thy name.
May Thy kingdom,
    there in obedient nature,
    there in the lives of the most obedient humans,
    and there in heaven,
    come here.
May thy will be endured, obeyed, and celebrated;
    may it be done, by me, now;
        I hereby submit to all future afflictions
    and I open myself to receive all future blessings.
Give us all we need for today.
Help us to go on forgiving and confessing;
    and help us to ignore an uneasy conscience or uneasy feelings
        which either vaguely accuse or vaguely approve
    and to go about our business.
Make straight our paths;
    and spare us, where possible, from all crises,

> *whether of temptation or affliction;*
> *and even from our previous prayers*
> *if we have asked anything*
> *which would be for us a snare or a sorrow.*
> *For thine is the sovereign goodness which claims my obedience,*
> *thine is the sovereign power,*
> *thine is the beauty so old and so new,*
> *and thine is the light from behind the sun.*
> *Amen.*

Letters to Malcolm: Chiefly on Prayer

LOVE

There is no safe investment. To love at all is to be vulnerable. Love anything, and your heart will certainly be wrung and possibly be broken. If you want to make sure of keeping it intact, you must give your heart to no one, not even to an animal. Wrap it carefully round with hobbies and little luxuries; avoid all entanglements; lock it up safe in the casket or coffin of your selfishness. But in that casket—safe, dark, motionless, airless—it will change. It will not be broken; it will become unbreakable, impenetrable, irredeemable. The alternative to tragedy, or at least to the risk of tragedy, is damnation. The only place outside Heaven where you can be perfectly safe from all the dangers and perturbations of love is Hell.

The Four Loves

Love is not affectionate feeling, but a steady wish for the loved person's ultimate good as far as it can be obtained.

God in the Dock

Even while we kill and punish we must try to feel about the enemy as we feel about ourselves—to wish that he were not bad, to hope that he may, in this world or another, be cured: in fact, to wish his good. That is what is meant in the Bible by loving him: wishing his good, not feeling fond of him nor saying he is nice when he is not.

Mere Christianity

There are two kinds of love: we love wise and kind and beautiful people because we need them, but we love (or try to love) stupid and disagreeable people because they need us. This second kind is the more divine because that is how God loves us: not because we are lovable but because He is love, not because He needs to receive but He delights to give.

The Collected Letters of C. S. Lewis, Volume III

Do not waste time bothering whether you "love" your neighbour; act as if you did. As soon as we do this we find one of the great secrets. When you are behaving as if you loved someone, you will presently come to love him. If you injure someone you dislike, you will find yourself disliking him more. If you do him a good turn, you will find yourself disliking him less. There is, indeed, one exception. If you do him a good turn, not to please God and obey the law of charity, but to show him what a fine forgiving chap you are and to put him in your debt, and then sit down to wait for his "gratitude," you will probably be disappointed. (People are not fools: they have a very quick eye for anything like showing off, or patronage.)

Mere Christianity

God will look to every soul like its first love because He is its first love.

The Problem of Pain

An old saint, being asked whether it is easy or hard to love God, replied: "It is easy *to those who do it.*"

Arthurian Torso

I will never laugh at anyone for grieving over a loved beast. I think God wants us to love Him more, not to love creatures (even animals) less. We love everything in one way too much (i.e., at the expense of our love for Him), but in another way we love everything too little.

No person, animal, flower, or even pebble has ever been loved too much—i.e., more than every one of God's works deserves.

The Collected Letters of C. S. Lewis, Volume III

It remains certainly true that all natural loves can be inordinate. Inordinate does not mean "insufficiently cautious." Nor does it mean "too big." It is not a quantitative term. It is probably impossible to love any human being simply "too much." We may love him too much in proportion to our love for God; but it is the smallness of our love for God, not the greatness of our love for the man, that constitutes the inordinacy.

The Four Loves

LUCK

"I say!" said Aravis. "I have had luck."

"Daughter," said the Hermit, "I have now lived a hundred and nine winters in this world and have never yet met any such thing as Luck. There is something about all this that I do not understand: but if ever we need to know it, you may be sure that we shall."

"I see," said Shasta to himself. "Those are the big mountains between Archenland and Narnia. I was on the other side of them yesterday. I must have come through the pass in the night. What luck that I hit it!—at least it wasn't luck at all really, it was Him. And now I'm in Narnia."

The Horse and His Boy

In the end Eustace and Jill begged so hard that Tirian said they could come with him and take their chance—or, as he much more sensibly called it, "the adventure that Aslan would send them."

The Last Battle

I am sure God has not forced B to give A the job. God's action wd. consist, I believe, in arranging all the circumstances so that A came at the right moment, etc.—i.e., in presenting B with the situation, on wh. then his free will worked. Ordinary people regard life as a mixture of "luck" and free will. It is the part usually called "luck" by which, on my view, God answers prayers.

The Collected Letters of C. S. Lewis, Volume II

MARRIAGE

Christian writers (notably Milton) have sometimes spoken of the husband's headship with a complacency to make the blood run cold. We must go back to our Bibles. The husband is the head of the wife just in so far as he is to her what Christ is to the Church. He is to love her as Christ loved the Church—read on—and give his life for her (Eph. V, 25). This headship, then, is most fully embodied not in the husband we should all wish to be but in him whose marriage is most like a crucifixion; whose wife receives most and gives least, is most unworthy of him—is in her own mere nature—least lovable.

The Four Loves

Aravis also had many quarrels (and, I'm afraid even fights) with Cor, but they always made it up again: so that years later, when they were grown up they were so used to quarrelling and making it up again that they got married so as to go on doing it more conveniently.

The Horse and His Boy

Justice, as I said before, includes the keeping of promises. Now everyone who has been married in a church has made a public, solemn promise to stick to his (or her) partner till death. The duty of keeping that promise has no special connection with sexual morality: it is in the same position as any other promise. If, as modern people are always telling us, the sexual impulse is just like all our other impulses, then it ought to be treated like all our other impulses; and as their indulgence is controlled by our promises, so should its be. If, as I think, it is not like all our other impulses, but is morbidly inflamed, then we should be especially careful not to let it lead us into dishonesty. . . .

If people do not believe in permanent marriage, it is perhaps better that they should live together unmarried than that they should make vows they do not mean to keep. It is true that by living together without marriage they will be guilty (in Christian eyes) of fornication. But one fault is not mended by adding another: unchastity is not improved by adding perjury.

Mere Christianity

Domesticity is no passport to heaven on earth but an arduous vocation—a sea full of hidden rocks and perilous ice shores only to be navigated by one who uses a celestial chart.

God in the Dock

MERE CHRISTIANITY

I hope no reader will suppose that "mere" Christianity is here put forward as an alternative to the creeds of the existing communions—as if a man could adopt it in preference to Congregationalism or Greek Orthodoxy or anything else. It is more like a hall out of which doors open into several rooms. If I can bring anyone into that hall I shall have done what I attempted.

Mere Christianity

The divisions of Christendom are undeniable and are by some of these writers most fiercely expressed. But if any man is tempted to think—as one might be tempted who read only contemporaries—that "Christianity" is a word of so many meanings that it means nothing at all, he can learn beyond all doubt, by stepping out of his own century, that this is not so. Measured against the ages "mere Christianity" turns out to be no insipid interdenominational transparency, but something positive, self-consistent, and inexhaustible. I know it, indeed, to my cost. In the days when I still hated Christianity, I learned to recognize, like some all too familiar smell, that almost unvarying something which met me, now in Puritan Bunyan, now in Anglican Hooker, now in Thomist Dante. It was there (honeyed and floral) in Francois de Sales; it was there (grave and homely) in Spenser and Walton; it was there (grim but manful) in Pascal and Johnson; there again, with a mild, frightening, Paradisial flavour, in Vaughan and Boehme and Traherne.

God in the Dock

MIRACLES

I use the word Miracle to mean an interference with Nature by supernatural power.

[Lewis's] Footnote: This definition is not that which would be given by many theologians. I am adopting it not because I think it an improvement upon theirs but precisely because, being crude and "popular," it enables me most easily to treat those questions which "the common reader" probably has in mind when he takes up a book on Miracles.

If the laws of Nature are necessary truths, no miracle can break them: but then no miracle needs to break them. It is with them as with the laws of arithmetic. If I put six pennies into a drawer on Monday and six more on Tuesday, the laws decree that other things being equal—I shall find twelve pennies there on Wednesday. But if the drawer has been robbed I may in fact find only two. Something will have been broken (the lock of the drawer or the laws of England) but the laws of arithmetic will not have been broken. The new situation created by the thief will illustrate the laws of arithmetic just as well as the original situation. But if God comes to work miracles, He comes "like a thief in the night." Miracle is, from the point of view of the scientists, a form of doctoring, tampering, (if you like) cheating. It introduces a new factor into the situation, namely supernatural force, which the scientists had not reckoned on.

All the essentials of Hinduism would, I think, remain unimpaired if you subtracted the miraculous, and the same is almost true of Mohammedanism. But you cannot do that with Christianity. It is precisely the story of a great Miracle. A naturalistic Christianity leaves out all that is specifically Christian.

Miracles

The miracle has only half its effect if it only convinces us that Christ is God: it will have its full effect if whenever we see a vineyard or drink a glass of wine we remember that here works He who sat at the wedding party in Cana.

God in the Dock

[In the miracles that fall in the class of Miracles of Fertility] are the two instances of miraculous feeding. They involve the multiplication of a little bread and a little fish into much bread and much fish. Once in the desert Satan had tempted Him to make bread of stones: He refused the suggestion. "The Son does nothing except what He sees the Father do"; perhaps one may without boldness surmise that the direct change from stone to bread appeared to the Son to be not quite in the hereditary style. Little bread into much bread is quite a different matter. Every year God makes a little corn into much corn: the seed is sown and there is an increase.

The idea that the progress of science has somehow altered this question is closely bound up with the idea that people "in olden times" believed in [miracles] "because they didn't know the laws of Nature." Thus you will hear people say, "The early Christians believed that Christ was the son of a virgin, but we know that this is a scientific impossibility." Such people seem to have an idea that belief in miracles arose at a period when men were so ignorant of the course of nature that they did not perceive a miracle to be contrary to it. A moment's thought shows this to be nonsense: and the story of the Virgin Birth is a particularly striking example. When St. Joseph discovered that his fiancée was going to have a baby, he not unnaturally decided to repudiate her. Why? Because he knew just as well as any modern gynaecologist that in the ordinary course of nature women do not have babies unless they have lain with men. No doubt the modern gynaecologist knows several things about birth and begetting which St. Joseph did not know. But those things do not concern the main point—that a virgin birth is contrary to the course of nature. And St. Joseph obviously knew that. In any sense in which it is true to say now, "The thing is scientifically impossible," he would have said the same: the thing always was, and was always known to be, impossible unless the regular processes of nature were, in this particular case, being over-ruled or supplemented by something from beyond nature. When St. Joseph finally accepted the view that his fiancée's pregnancy was due not to unchastity but to a miracle, he accepted the miracle as something contrary to the known order of nature. All records of miracles teach the same thing. In such stories the miracles excite fear and wonder (that is what the very word miracle implies) among the spectators, and are taken as evidence of supernatural power. If they were not known to be contrary to the laws of nature how could they suggest the presence of the supernatural? How could they be surprising unless they were seen to be exceptions to the rules? And how can anything be seen to be an exception till the rules are known?

If there ever were men who did not know the laws of nature at all, they would have no idea of a miracle and feel no particular interest in one if it were performed before them. Nothing can seem extraordinary until you have discovered what is ordinary. Belief in miracles, far from depending on an ignorance of the laws of nature, is only possible in so far as those laws are known. We have already seen that if you begin by ruling out the supernatural you will perceive no miracles. We must now add that you will equally perceive no miracles until you believe that nature works according to regular laws. If you have not yet noticed that the sun always rises in the East you will see nothing miraculous about his rising one morning in the West.

Miracles

MORALITY

A world of nice people, content in their own niceness, looking no further, turned away from God, would be just as desperately in need of salvation as a miserable world—and might even be more difficult to save.

There are . . . occasions on which a mother's love for her own children or a man's love for his own country have to be suppressed or they'll lead to unfairness toward other people's children or countries. Strictly speaking, there aren't such things as good and bad impulses. Think of a piano. It has not got two kinds of notes on it, the right notes and the wrong ones. Every single note is right at one time and wrong at another. The moral law isn't any one instinct or any set of instincts: it is something which makes a kind of tune (the tune we call goodness or right conduct) by directing the instincts. . . .

The most dangerous thing you can do is to take any one impulse of your own nature and set it up as the thing you ought to follow at all costs. There's not one of them that won't make us into devils if we set it up as an absolute guide. You might think love of humanity in general was safe, but it isn't. If you leave out justice, you'll find yourself breaking agreements and faking evidence in trials "for the sake of humanity," and becoming in the end a treacherous man.

Mere Christianity

The very idea of freedom presupposes some objective moral law which overarches rulers and ruled alike. . . . Unless we return to the crude and nursery-like belief in objective values, we perish. If we do, we may live, and such a return might have one minor advantage. If we believed in the absolute reality of elementary moral platitudes, we should value those who solicit our votes by other standards than have recently been in fashion. While we believe that good is something to be invented, we demand of our rulers such qualities as "vision," "dynamism," "creativity," and the like. If we returned to the objective view we should demand qualities much rarer, and much more beneficial—virtue, knowledge, diligence and skill. "Vision" is for sale, or claims to be for sale, everywhere. But give me a man who will do a day's work for a day's pay, who will refuse bribes, who will not make up his facts, and who has learned his job.

Christian Reflections

God may be more than moral goodness: He is not less. The road to the promised land runs past Sinai. The moral law may exist to be transcended: but there is no transcending it for those who have not first admitted its claims upon them, and then tried with all their strength to meet that claim, and fairly and squarely faced the fact of their failure.

The Problem of Pain

I think all Christians would agree with me if I said that though Christianity seems at first to be all about morality, all about duties and rules and guilt and virtue, yet it leads you on, out of all that, into something beyond. One has a glimpse of a country where they do not talk of those things, except perhaps as a joke. Everyone there is filled full with what we should call goodness as a mirror is filled with light. But they do not call it goodness. They do not call it anything. They are not thinking of it. They are too busy looking at the source from which it comes. But this is near the stage where the road passes over the rim of our world. No one's eyes can see very far beyond that: lots of people's eyes can see further than mine.

Mere Christianity

NEIGHBOR

It may be possible for each to think too much of his own potential glory hereafter; it is hardly possible for him to think too often or too deeply about that of his neighbour. The load, or weight, or burden of my neighbour's glory should be laid daily on my back, a load so heavy that only humility can carry it, and the backs of the proud will be broken. It is a serious thing to live in a society of possible gods and goddesses, to remember that the dullest and most uninteresting person you can talk to may one day be a creature which, if you saw it now, you would be strongly tempted to worship, or else a horror and a corruption such as you now meet, if at all, only in a nightmare.

The Weight of Glory

Now that I come to think of it, I have not exactly got a feeling of fondness or affection for myself, and I do not even always enjoy my own society. So apparently "Love your neighbour" does not mean "feel fond of him" or "find him attractive." I ought to have seen that before, because, of course, you cannot feel fond of a person by trying. Do I think well of myself, think myself a nice chap? Well, I am afraid I sometimes do (and those are, no doubt, my worst moments) but that is not why I love myself. In fact it is the other way round: my self-love makes me think myself nice, but thinking myself nice is not why I love myself. So loving my enemies does not apparently mean thinking them nice either. That is an enormous relief.

Mere Christianity

OBEDIENCE

In obeying, a rational creature consciously enacts its creaturely role, reverses the act by which we fell, treads Adam's dance backward and returns.

The Problem of Pain

"Regular but cool" in Church attendance is no bad symptom. Obedience is the key to all doors; feelings come (or don't come) and go as God pleases. We can't produce them at will, and mustn't try.

The Collected Letters of C. S. Lewis, Volume III

OMNIPOTENCE

Omnipotence means "power to do all, or everything." And we are told in Scripture that "with God all things are possible." It is common enough, in argument with an unbeliever, to be told that God, if He existed and were good, would do this or that; and then, if we point out that the proposed action is impossible, to be met with the retort, "But I thought God was supposed to be able to do anything." This raises the whole question of impossibility.

In ordinary usage the word impossible generally implies a suppressed clause beginning with the word unless. Thus it is impossible for me to see the street from where I sit writing at this moment; that is, it is impossible to see the street unless I go up to the top floor where I shall be high enough to overlook the intervening building. If I had broken my leg I should say "But it is impossible to go up to the top floor"—meaning, however, that it is impossible unless some friends turn up who will carry me. Now let us advance to a different plane of impossibility, by saying "It is, at any rate, impossible to see the street so long as I remain where I am and the intervening building remains where it is." Someone might add "unless the nature of space, or of vision, were different from what it is." I do not know what the best philosophers and scientists would say to this, but I should have to reply "I don't know whether space and vision could possibly have been of such a nature as you suggest." Now it is clear that the words could possibly here refer to some absolute kind of possibility or impossibility which is different from the relative possibilities and impossibilities we have been considering. I cannot say whether seeing round corners is, in this new sense, possible or not, because I do not know whether it is self-contradictory or not. But I know very well that if it is self-contradictory it is absolutely impossible. The absolutely impossible may also be called the intrinsically impossible because it carries its impossibility within itself, instead of borrowing it from other impossibilities which in their turn depend upon others. It has no "unless" clause attached to it. It is impossible under all conditions and in all worlds and for all agents.

The Problem of Pain

PAIN

When pain is to be borne, a little courage helps more than much knowledge, a little human sympathy more than much courage, and the least tincture of the love of God more than all.

Try to exclude the possibility of suffering which the order of nature and the existence of free-wills involve, and you find that you have excluded life itself.

The Problem of Pain

I have not a word to say against the doctrine that Our Lord suffers in all the suffering of His people (see Acts IX. 6) or that when we willingly accept what we suffer for others and offer it to God on their behalf, then it may be united with His sufferings and, in Him, may help to their redemption or even that of others whom we do not dream of. So that it is not in vain; tho' of course we must not count on seeing it work out exactly as we, in our present ignorance, might think best. The key text for this view is Colossians I. 24. Is it not, after all, one more application of the truth that we are all "members one of another"? I wish I had known more when I wrote *Problem of Pain*.

That suffering is not always sent as a punishment is clearly established for believers by the book of Job and by John IX. 1–4. That it sometimes is, is suggested by parts of the Old Testament and Revelation. It wd. certainly be most dangerous to assume that any given pain was penal. I believe that all pain is contrary to God's will, absolutely but not relatively. When I am taking a thorn out of my finger (or a child's finger) the pain is "absolutely" contrary to my will: i.e., if I could have chosen a situation without pain I would have done so. But I do will what caused pain, relatively to the given situation: i.e., granted the thorn I prefer the pain to leaving the thorn where it is. A mother smacking a child wd. be in the same position: she wd. rather cause it this pain than let it go on pulling the cat's tail, but she wd. like it better if no situation which demands a smack had arisen.

The Collected Letters of C. S. Lewis, Volume III

But Job's impatience had been approved. His apparent blasphemies had been accepted. The weight of the divine displeasure had been reserved for the "comforters," the self-appointed advocates on God's side, the people who tried to show that all was well— "the sort of people," he said, immeasurably dropping his lower jaw and fixing me with his eyes—"the sort of people who wrote books on the Problem of Pain."

Essays Presented to Charles Williams

PATIENCE

William Law remarks that people are merely "amusing themselves" by asking for the patience which a famine or a persecution would call for if, in the meantime, the weather and every other inconvenience sets them grumbling. One must learn to walk before one can run.

Letters to Malcolm: Chiefly on Prayer

How right you are to see that anger (even when directed against oneself) "worketh not the righteousness of God." One must never be either content with, or impatient with, oneself. My old confessor (now dead) used to impress on me the need for the 3 Patiences: patience with God, with my neighbour, with oneself.

The Collected Letters of C. S. Lewis, Volume III

I have seen great beauty of spirit in some who were great sufferers. I have seen men, for the most part, grow better, not worse, with advancing years, and I have seen the last illness produce treasures of fortitude and meekness from most unpromising subjects. I see in loved and revered historical figures, such as Johnson and Cowper, traits which might scarcely have been tolerable if the men had been happier. If the world is indeed a "vale of soul making" it seems on the whole to be doing its work. Of poverty—the affliction which actually or potentially includes all other afflictions—I would not dare to speak as from myself; and those who reject Christianity will not be moved by Christ's statement that poverty is blessed. But here a rather remarkable fact comes to my aid. Those who would most scornfully repudiate Christianity as a mere "opiate of the people" have a contempt for the rich, that is, for all mankind except the poor. They regard the poor as the only people worth preserving from "liquidation," and place in them the only hope of the human race. But this is not compatible with a belief that the effects of poverty on those who suffer it are wholly evil; it even implies that they are good. The Marxist thus finds himself in real agreement with the Christian in those two beliefs which Christianity paradoxically demands—that poverty is blessed and yet ought to be removed.

The Problem of Pain

What meditation on human fate demands so much "courage" as the act of stepping into a cold bath? I should be glad to hear of it, for I know no path to heroism which sounds so suited to my own capacities.

The Personal Heresy

[The demon Screwtape writes:] Your patient will, of course, have picked up the notion that he must submit with patience to the Enemy's will. What the Enemy means by this is primarily that he should accept with patience the tribulation which has actually been dealt out to him—the present anxiety and suspense. It is about this that he is to say "Thy will be done," and for the daily task of bearing this that the daily bread will be provided. It is your business to see that the patient never thinks of the present fear as his appointed cross but only of the things he is afraid of. Let him regard them as his crosses: let him forget that, since they are incompatible, they cannot all happen to him, and let him try to practise fortitude and patience to them all in advance. For real resignation, at the same moment, to a dozen different and hypothetical fates is almost impossible, and the Enemy does not greatly assist those who are trying to attain it: resignation to present and actual suffering, even where that suffering consists of fear, is far easier and is usually helped by this direct action.

The Screwtape Letters

PERFECTION

The command *Be ye perfect* is not idealistic gas. Nor is it a command to do the impossible. He is going to make us into creatures that can obey that command. He said (in the Bible) that we were "gods" and He is going to make good His words. If we let Him—for we can prevent Him, if we choose—He will make the feeblest and filthiest of us into a god or goddess, a dazzling, radiant, immortal creature, pulsating all through with such energy and joy and wisdom and love as we cannot now imagine, a bright stainless mirror which reflects back to God perfectly (though, of course, on a smaller scale) His own boundless power and delight and goodness. The process will be long and in parts very painful; but that is what we are in for. Nothing less. He meant what He said.

Mere Christianity

Christ has risen, and so we shall rise. St. Peter for a few seconds walked on the water; and the day will come when there will be a re-made universe, infinitely obedient to the will of glorified and obedient men, when we can do all things, when we shall be those gods that we are described as being in Scripture.

Morality is indispensable: but the Divine Life, which gives itself to us and which calls us to be gods, intends for us something in which morality will be swallowed up. We are to be re-made. All the rabbit in us is to disappear—the worried, conscientious, ethical rabbit as well as the cowardly and sensual rabbit. We shall bleed and squeal as the handfuls of fur come out; and then, surprisingly, we shall find underneath it all a thing we have never yet imagined: a real Man, an ageless god, a son of God, strong, radiant, wise, beautiful, and drenched in joy.

God in the Dock

PLEASURE

[The demon Screwtape writes:] [God, the "Enemy," is] a hedonist at heart. All those fasts and vigils and stakes and crosses are only a facade. Or only like foam on the sea shore. Out at sea, out in His sea, there is pleasure, and more pleasure. He makes no secret of it; at His right hand are "pleasures for evermore." Ugh! Don't think He has the least inkling of that high and austere mystery to which we rise in the Miserific Vision. He's vulgar, Wormwood. He has a bourgeois mind. He has filled His world full of pleasures. There are things for humans to do all day long without His minding in the least—sleeping, washing, eating, drinking, making love, playing, praying, working. Everything has to be twisted before it's any use to us. We fight under cruel disadvantages. Nothing is naturally on our side.

The Screwtape Letters

But aren't there bad, unlawful pleasures? Certainly there are. But in calling them "bad pleasures" I take it we are using a kind of shorthand. We mean "pleasures snatched by unlawful acts." It is the stealing of the apple that is bad, not the sweetness. The sweetness is still a beam from the glory. That does not palliate the stealing. It makes it worse. There is sacrilege in the theft. We have abused a holy thing. I have tried . . . to make every pleasure into a channel of adoration. I don't mean simply by giving thanks for it. . . . We can't—or I can't—hear the song of a bird simply as a sound. Its meaning or message ("That's a bird") comes with it inevitably—just as one can't see a familiar word in print as a merely visual pattern. The reading is as involuntary as the seeing. When the wind roars I don't just hear the roar; I "hear the wind." In the same way it is possible to "read" as well as to "have" a pleasure. Or not even "as well as." The distinction ought to become, and sometimes is, impossible; to receive it and to recognise its divine source are a single experience. This heavenly fruit is instantly redolent of the orchard where it grew. This sweet air whispers of the country from whence it blows. It is a message. We know we are being touched by a finger of that right hand at which there are pleasures for evermore.

Letters to Malcolm: Chiefly on Prayer

Looking round he perceived innumerable shimmering globes of the same kind in every direction. He began to examine the nearest one attentively. At first he thought it was moving, then he thought it was not. Moved by a natural impulse he put out his hand to touch it. Immediately his head, face, and shoulders were drenched with what seemed (in that warm world) an ice-cold shower bath, and his nostrils filled with a sharp, shrill, exquisite scent that somehow brought to his mind the verse in Pope, "die of a rose in aromatic pain." Such was the refreshment that he seemed to himself to have been, till now, but half awake. When he opened his eyes—which had closed involuntarily at the shock of moisture—all the colours about him seemed richer and the dimness of that world seemed clarified. A re-enchantment fell upon him. . . . He turned again to the tree. The thing that had drenched him was quite vanished. The tube or branch, deprived of its pendent globe, now ended in a little quivering orifice from which there hung a bead of crystal moisture.

He looked round in some bewilderment. The grove was still full of its iridescent fruit but now he perceived that there was a slow continual movement. A second later he had mastered the phenomenon. Each of the bright spheres was very gradually increasing in size, and each, on reaching a certain dimension, vanished with a faint noise, and in its place there was a momentary dampness on the soil and a soon-fading, delicious fragrance and coldness in the air. In fact, the things were not fruit at all but bubbles. The trees (he christened them at that moment) were bubble-trees. Their life, apparently, consisted in drawing up water from the ocean and then expelling it in this form, but enriched by its short sojourn in their sappy inwards. He sat down to feed his eyes upon the spectacle. Now that he knew the secret he could explain to himself why this wood looked and felt so different from every other part of the island. Each bubble, looked at individually could be seen to emerge from its parent-branch as a mere bead, the size of a pea, and swell and burst; but looking at the wood as a whole, one was conscious only of a continual faint disturbance of light, an elusive interference with the prevailing Perelandrian silence, an unusual coolness in the air, and a fresher quality in the perfume. To a man born in our world it felt a more out-door place than the open parts of the island, or even the sea. Looking at a fine cluster of the bubbles which hung above his head, he thought how easy it would be to get up and plunge oneself through the whole lot of them and to feel, all at once, that magical refreshment multiplied tenfold. But he was restrained by the same sort of feeling which had restrained him over-night from tasting a second gourd.

Perelandra

PRAISE

The Jews, like nearly all the ancients, were agricultural and approached Nature with a gardener's and a farmer's interest, concerned with rain, with grass "for the service of man," wine to cheer man up and olive-oil to make his face shine—to make it look, as Homer says somewhere, like a peeled onion ([Ps.] 104, 14, 15). But we find them led on beyond this. Their gusto, or even gratitude, embraces things that are no use to man. In the great Psalm especially devoted to Nature, from which I have just quoted (104), we have not only the useful cattle, the cheering vine, and the nourishing corn, we have springs where the wild asses quench their thirst (11), fir trees for the storks (17), hill country for the wild goats and "conies" (perhaps marmots, 18), finally even the lions (21); and even with a glance far out to sea, where no Jew willingly went, the great whales playing, enjoying themselves (26).

I think we delight to praise what we enjoy because the praise not merely expresses but completes the enjoyment; it is its appointed consummation.

Reflections on the Psalms

We all sin by needlessly disobeying the apostolic injunction to rejoice as much as by anything else.

The Problem of Pain

PRAYER

Mr. Wirt: What is your view of the daily discipline of the Christian life—the need for taking time to be alone with God?

Lewis: We have our New Testament regimental orders upon the subject. I would take it for granted that everyone who becomes a Christian would undertake this practice. It is enjoined upon us by Our Lord; and since they are His commands, I believe in following them. It is always just possible that Jesus Christ meant what He said when He told us to seek the secret place and to close the door.

God in the Dock

"I was wondering—I mean—could there be some mistake? Because nobody called me and Scrubb, you know. It was we who asked to come here. Scrubb said we were to call to—to Somebody—it was a name I wouldn't know—and perhaps the Somebody would let us in. And we did, and then we found the door open."

"You would not have called to me unless I had been calling to you," said the Lion.

The Silver Chair

We are like earthworms, cabbages, and nebulae, objects of divine knowledge. But when we (a) become aware of the fact—the present fact, not the generalisation—and (b) assent with all our will to be so known, then we treat ourselves, in relation to God, not as things but as persons. We have unveiled. Not that any veil could have baffled this sight. The change is in us. The passive changes to the active. Instead of merely being known, we show, we tell, we offer ourselves to view.

Letters to Malcolm: Chiefly on Prayer

"Praying for particular things," said I, "always seems to me like advising God how to run the world. Wouldn't it be wiser to assume that He knows best?" "On the same principle," said he, "I suppose you never ask a man next to you to pass the salt, because God knows best whether you ought to have salt or not. And I suppose you never take an umbrella, because God knows best whether you ought to be wet or dry." "That's quite different," I protested. "I don't see why," said he. "The odd thing is that He should let us influence the course of events at all. But since He lets us do it in one way I don't see why He shouldn't let us do it in the other."

God in the Dock

One of the purposes for which God instituted prayer may have been to bear witness that the course of events is not governed like a state but created like a work of art to which every being makes its contribution and (in prayer) a conscious contribution, and in which every being is both an end and a means.

Letters to Malcolm: Chiefly on Prayer

The kind of causality we exercise by work is, so to speak, divinely guaranteed, and therefore ruthless. By it we are free to do ourselves as much harm as we please. But the kind which we exercise by prayer is not like that; God has left Himself a discretionary power. Had

He not done so, prayer would be an activity too dangerous for man and we should have the horrible state of things envisaged by Juvenal: "Enormous prayers which Heaven in anger grants.". . .

Prayers are not always—in the crude, factual sense of the word—"granted." This is not because prayer is a weaker kind of causality, but because it is a stronger kind. When it "works" at all it works unlimited by space and time. That is why God has retained a discretionary power of granting or refusing it; except on that condition prayer would destroy us. It is not unreasonable for a headmaster to say, "Such and such things you may do according to the fixed rules of this school. But such and such other things are too dangerous to be left to general rules. If you want to do them you must come and make a request and talk over the whole matter with me in my study. And then—we'll see."

God in the Dock

The very question "Does prayer work?" puts us in the wrong frame of mind from the outset. "Work": as if it were magic, or a machine—something that functions automatically. Prayer is either a sheer illusion or a personal contact between embryonic, incomplete persons (ourselves) and the utterly concrete Person. Prayer in the sense of petition, asking for things, is a small part of it; confession and penitence are its threshold, adoration its sanctuary, the presence and vision and enjoyment of God its bread and wine. In it God shows Himself to us. That He answers prayers is a corollary—not necessarily the most important one—from that revelation. What He does is learned from what He is.

The World's Last Night

"Whether it is any good praying for actual things"—the first question is what one means by "any good." Is it a good thing to do? Yes: however we explain it, we are told to ask for particular things such as our daily bread. Does it "work"? Certainly not like a mechanical operation or a magical spell. It is a request which of course the Other Party may or may not, for His own good reasons, grant. But how can it change God's will? Well—but how v. odd it would be if God in His actions towards me were bound to ignore what I did (including my prayers). Surely He hasn't to forgive me for sins I didn't commit or to cure me of errors into which I have never fallen! In other words His will (however changeless in some ultimate metaphysical sense) must be related to what I am and do? And once grant that, and why should my asking or not asking not be one of the things He takes into account? At any rate He said He would—and He ought to know. (We often talk as if He were not very good at Theology!)

The Collected Letters of C. S. Lewis, Volume III

Meantime, however, we want to know not how we should pray if we were perfect but how we should pray being as we now are. And if my idea of prayer as "unveiling" is accepted, we have already answered this. It is no use to ask God with factitious earnestness for A when our whole mind is in reality filled with the desire for B. We must lay before Him what is in us, not what ought to be in us. . . .

It may well be that the desire can be laid before God only as a sin to be repented; but one of the best ways of learning this is to lay it before God. . . . I have no doubt at all that if they [our desires] are the subject of our thoughts they must be the subject of our prayers—whether in penitence or in petition or in a little of both: penitence for the excess, yet petition for the thing we desire.

I would rather say that from before all worlds His providential and creative act (for they are all one) takes into account all the situations produced by the acts of His creatures. And if He takes our sins into account, why not our petitions?

Letters to Malcolm: Chiefly on Prayer

"Well, I do think someone might have arranged about our meals," said Digory.

"I'm sure Aslan would have, if you'd asked him," said Fledge.

"Wouldn't he know without being asked?" said Polly.

"I've no doubt he would," said the Horse (still with his mouth full). "But I've a sort of idea he likes to be asked."

The Magician's Nephew

Prayer is request. The essence of request, as distinct from compulsion, is that it may or may not be granted. And if an infinitely wise Being listens to the requests of finite and foolish creatures, of course He will sometimes grant and sometimes refuse them. Invariable "success" in prayer would not prove the Christian doctrine at all. It would prove something much more like magic—a power in certain human beings to control, or compel, the course of nature.

The World's Last Night

I am often, I believe, praying for others when I should be doing things for them. It's so much easier to pray for a bore than to go and see him.

Letters to Malcolm: Chiefly on Prayer

PRESENCE OF GOD

When any man comes into the presence of God he will find, whether he wishes it or not, that all those things which seemed to make him so different from the men of other times, or even from his earlier self, have fallen off him. He is back where he always was, where every man always is. *Eadem sunt omnia simper* ["Everything is always the same"]. Do not let us deceive ourselves. No possible complexity which we can give to our picture of the universe can hide us from God: there is no copse, no forest, no jungle thick enough to provide cover. We read in Revelation of Him that sat on the throne "from whose face the earth and heaven fled away." It may happen to any of us at any moment. In the twinkling of an eye, in a time too small to be measured, and in any place, all that seems to divide us from God can flee away, vanish, leaving us naked before Him, like the first man, like the only man, as if nothing but He and I existed. And since that contact cannot be avoided for long, and since it means either bliss or horror, the business of life is to learn to like it.

God in the Dock

If we cannot "practice the presence of God," it is something to practice the absence of God, to become increasingly aware of our unawareness till we feel like men who should stand beside a great cataract and hear no noise, or like a man in a story who looks in a mirror and finds no face there, or a man in a dream who stretches out his hand to visible objects and gets no sensation of touch. To know that one is dreaming is to be no longer perfectly asleep.

The Four Loves

We may ignore, but we can nowhere evade, the presence of God. The world is crowded with Him. He walks everywhere incognito. And the incognito is not always hard to penetrate. The real labour is to remember, to attend. In fact, to come awake. Still more, to remain awake.

Letters to Malcolm: Chiefly on Prayer

To believe that God—at least *this* God—exists is to believe that you as a person now stand in the presence of God as a Person. What would, a moment before, have been variations in opinion, now becomes variations in your personal attitude to a Person. You are no longer faced with an argument which demands your assent, but with a Person who demands your confidence.

The World's Last Night

PRESENT MOMENT

God is hearing you now, just as simply as a mother hears a child. The difference His timelessness makes is that this now (which slips away from you even as you say the word now) is for Him infinite. If you must think of His timelessness at all, don't think of Him having looked forward to this moment for millions of years: think that to Him you are always praying this prayer.

The Collected Letters of C. S. Lewis, Volume II

This moment contains all moments.

The Great Divorce

Never, in peace or war, commit your virtue or your happiness to the future. Happy work is best done by the man who takes his long-term plans somewhat lightly and works from moment to moment "as to the Lord." It is only our daily bread that we are encouraged to ask for. The present is the only time in which any duty can be done or any grace received.

The Weight of Glory

PRIDE

According to Christian teachers, the essential vice, the utmost evil, is Pride. Unchastity, anger, greed, drunkenness, and all that are mere fleabites in comparison: it was through Pride that the devil became the devil: Pride leads to every other vice: it is the complete anti-God state of mind. . . .

Now what you want to get clear is that Pride is essentially competitive—is competitive by its very nature—while the other vices are competitive only, so to speak, by accident. Pride gets no pleasure out of having something, only out of having more of it than the next man.

As long as you are proud you cannot know God. A proud man is always looking down on things and people: and, of course, as long as you are looking down, you cannot see something that is above you.

Pride is spiritual cancer; it eats the very possibility of love or contentment, or even common sense.

Before leaving [the] subject [of pride] I must guard against some possible misunderstandings:

Pleasure in being praised is not Pride. The child who is patted on the back for doing a lesson well, the woman whose beauty is praised by her lover, the saved soul to whom Christ says "Well done," are pleased and ought to be. For here the pleasure lies not in what you are but in the fact that you have pleased someone you wanted (and rightly wanted) to please. The trouble begins when you pass from thinking, "I have pleased him; all is well," to thinking, "What a fine person I must be to have done it." The more you delight in yourself and the less you delight in the praise, the worse you are becoming. When you delight wholly in yourself and do not care about the praise at all, you have reached the bottom. That is why vanity, though it is the sort of Pride which shows most on the surface, is really the least bad and most pardonable sort. The vain person wants praise, applause, admiration, too much and is always angling for it. It is a fault, but a childlike and even (in an odd way) a humble fault. It shows that you are not yet completely contented with your own admiration. You value other people enough to want them to look at you. You are, in fact, still human. The real black, diabolical Pride comes when you look down on others so much that you do not care what they think of you. Of course, it is very right, and often our duty, not to care what people think of us, if we do so for the right reason; namely, because we care so incomparably more what God thinks. But the Proud man has a different reason for not caring. He says "Why should I care for the applause of that rabble as if their opinion were worth anything? And even if their opinions were of value, am I the sort of man to blush with pleasure at a compliment like some chit of a girl at her first dance? No, I am an integrated, adult personality. All I have done has been done to satisfy my own ideals—or my artistic conscience— or the traditions of my family—or, in a word, because I'm That Kind of Chap. If the mob like it, let them. They're nothing to me." In this way real thoroughgoing Pride may act as a check on vanity; for, as I said a moment ago, the devil loves "curing" a small fault by giving you a great one. We must try not to be vain, but we must never call in our Pride to cure our vanity; better the frying-pan than the fire.

We say in English that a man is "proud" of his son, or his father, or his school, or regiment, and it may be asked whether "pride" in this sense is a sin. I think it depends on what, exactly, we mean by "proud of." Very often, in such sentences, the phrase "is proud of" means "has a warm-hearted admiration for." Such an admiration is, of course, very far from being a sin. But it might, perhaps, mean that the person in question gives himself airs on the ground of his distinguished father, or because he belongs to a famous regiment. This would, clearly, be a fault; but even then, it would be better than being proud simply of himself. To love and admire anything outside yourself is to take one step away from utter spiritual ruin; though we shall not be well so long as we love and admire anything more than we love and admire God.

We must not think Pride is something God forbids because He is offended at it, or that Humility is something He demands as due to His own dignity—as if God Himself was proud. He is not in the least worried about His dignity. The point is, He wants you to know Him: wants to give you Himself. And He and you are two things of such a kind that if you really get into any kind of touch with Him you will, in fact, be humble—delightedly humble, feeling the infinite relief of having for once got rid of all the silly nonsense about your own dignity which has made you restless and unhappy all your life. He is trying to make you humble in order to make this moment possible: trying to take off a lot of silly, ugly, fancy-dress in which we have all got ourselves up and are strutting about like the little idiots we are. I wish I had got a bit further with humility myself: if I had, I could probably tell you more about the relief, the comfort, of taking the fancy-dress off—getting rid of the false self, with all its "Look at me" and "Aren't I a good boy?" and all its posing and posturing. To get even near it, even for a moment, is like a drink of cold water to a man in a desert.

Mere Christianity

PROVIDENCE

As to "Fate," which I call providence—I believe that the coming together of a man and woman, like everything else (e.g., the fall of [a] sparrow) is in the hand of God.

The Collected Letters of C. S. Lewis, Volume II

Oh what a rare blessing to have a Christian psychotherapist! I don't think yr. question whether these ones were brought into your life by "a whimsical fate" or by God need detain you long. Once one believes in God at all, surely the question is meaningless? Suppose that in a novel a character gets killed in a railway accident. Is his death due to chance (e.g., the signals being wrong) or to the novelist? Well of course, both. The chance is the way the novelist removes the character at the exact moment his story requires. There's a good line in Spenser to quote to oneself: "It chanced (almighty God that chance did guide)."

The Collected Letters of C. S. Lewis, Volume III

In Friendship . . . we think we have chosen our peers. In reality, a few years' difference in the dates of our births, a few more miles between certain houses, the choice of one university instead of another, posting to different regiments, the accident of a topic being raised or not raised at a first meeting—any of these chances might have kept us apart. But, for a Christian, there are, strictly speaking, no chances. A secret Master of the Ceremonies has been at work. Christ, who said to the disciples "Ye have not chosen me, but I have chosen you," can truly say to every group of Christian friends "You have not chosen one another but I have chosen you for one another."

The Four Loves

"I was the lion." And as Shasta gaped with open mouth and said nothing, the Voice continued. "I was the lion who forced you to join with Aravis. I was the cat who comforted you among the houses of the dead. I was the lion who drove the jackals from you while you slept. I was the lion who gave the Horses the new strength of fear for the last mile so that you should reach King Lune in time. And I was the lion you do not remember who pushed the boat in which you lay, a child near death, so that it came to shore where a man sat, wakeful at midnight, to receive you."

"Then it was you who wounded Aravis?"

"It was I."

"But what for?"

"Child," said the Voice, "I am telling you your story, not hers. I tell no-one any story but his own."

The Horse and His Boy

"And we saw the words UNDER ME."

The Knight laughed even more heartily than before. "You were the more deceived," he said. "Those words meant nothing to your purpose. Had you but asked my Lady, she could have given you better counsel. For those words are all that is left of a longer script, which in ancient times, as she well remembers, expressed this verse:

Though under Earth and throneless now I be,
Yet, while I lived, all Earth was under me.

From which it is plain that some great king of the ancient giants who lies buried there caused this boast to be cut in the stone over his sepulchre; though the breaking up of some stones, and the carrying away of others for new buildings, and the filling up of the cuts with rubble has left only two words that can still be read. Is it not the merriest jest in the world that you should have thought they were written to you?"

This was like cold water down the back to Scrubb and Jill; for it seemed to them very likely that the words had nothing to do with their quest at all, and that they had been taken in by a mere accident.

"Don't you mind," said Puddleglum. "There are no accidents. Our guide is Aslan."

The Silver Chair

PURGATORY

I have a notion that, apart from actual pain, men and women are quite diversely affected by illness. To a woman one of the great evils about it is that she can't do things. To a man (or anyway a man like me) the great consolation is the reflection "Well, anyway, no one can now demand that I should do anything." I have often had the fancy that one stage in Purgatory might be a great big kitchen in which things are always going wrong—milk boiling over, crockery getting smashed, toast burning, animals stealing. The women have to learn to sit still and mind their own business: the men have to learn to jump up and do something about it. When both sexes have mastered this exercise, they go on to the next.

The Collected Letters of C. S. Lewis, Volume III

I believe in Purgatory.

Mind you, the Reformers had good reasons for throwing doubt on "the Romish doctrine concerning Purgatory" as that Romish doctrine had then become. I don't mean merely the commercial scandal. If you turn from Dante's *Purgatorio* to the sixteenth century you will be appalled by the degradation. In Thomas More's *Supplication of Souls* Purgatory is simply temporary Hell. In it the souls are tormented by devils, whose presence is "more horrible and grievous to us than is the pain itself." Worse still, Fisher, in his *Sermon on Psalm VI,* says the tortures are so intense that the spirit who suffers them cannot, for pain, "remember God as he ought to do." In fact, the very etymology of the word purgatory has dropped out of sight. Its pains do not bring us nearer to God, but make us forget Him. It is a place not of purification but purely of retributive punishment.

The right view returns magnificently in Newman's *Dream*. There, if I remember it rightly, the saved soul, at the very foot of the throne, begs to be taken away and cleansed. It cannot bear for a moment longer "With its darkness to affront that light." Religion has reclaimed Purgatory.

Our souls demand Purgatory, don't they? Would it not break the heart if God said to us, "It is true, my son, that your breath smells and your rags drip with mud and slime, but we are charitable here and no one will upbraid you with these things, nor draw away from you. Enter into the joy"? Should we not reply, "With submission, sir, and if there is no objection, I'd rather be cleaned first." "It may hurt, you know"—"Even so, sir."

I assume that the process of purification will normally involve suffering. Partly from tradition; partly because most real good that has been done me in this life has involved it. But I don't think suffering is the purpose of the purgation. I can well believe that people neither much worse nor much better than I will suffer less than I or more. "No nonsense about merit." The treatment given will be the one required, whether it hurts little or much.

My favourite image on this matter comes from the dentist's chair. I hope that when the tooth of life is drawn and I am "coming round," a voice will say, "Rinse your mouth out with this."

This will be Purgatory. The rinsing may take longer than I can now imagine. The taste of this may be more fiery and astringent than my present sensibility could endure. But More and Fisher shall not persuade me that it will be disgusting and unhallowed.

Letters to Malcolm: Chiefly on Prayer

REASON

All possible knowledge, then, depends on the validity of reasoning. If the feeling of certainty which we express by words like must be and therefore and since is a real perception of how things outside our own minds really "must" be, well and good. But if this certainty is merely a feeling in our own minds and not a genuine insight into realities beyond them—if it merely represents the way our minds happen to work—then we can have no knowledge. Unless human reasoning is valid no science can be true. It follows that no account of the universe can be true unless that account leaves it possible for our thinking to be a real insight. A theory which explained everything else in the whole universe but which made it impossible to believe that our thinking was valid would be utterly out of court. For that theory would itself have been reached by thinking, and if thinking is not valid that theory would, of course, be itself demolished. It would have destroyed its own credentials. It would be an argument which proved that no argument was sound—a proof that there are no such things as proofs—which is nonsense.

Every object you see before you at this moment—the walls, ceiling, and furniture, the book, your own washed hands and cut fingernails—bears witness to the colonisation of Nature by Reason: for none of this matter would have been in these states if Nature had had her way.

Miracles

THE METEORITE

Among the hills a meteorite
Lies huge; and moss has overgrown,
And wind and rain with touches light
Made soft, the contours of the stone.
Thus easily can Earth digest
A cinder of sidereal fire,
And make the translunary guest
Thus native to an English shire.
Nor is it strange these wanderers
Find in her lap their fitting place,
For every particle that's hers
Came at the first from outer space.
All that is Earth has once been sky;
Down from the Sun of old she came,
Or from some star that travelled by
Too close to his entangling flame.
Hence, if belated drops yet fall
From heaven, on these her plastic power
Still works as once it worked on all
The glad rush of the golden shower.

The Collected Poems of C. S. Lewis

Let us go back to the question of Logic. I have tried to show that you reach a self-contradiction if you say that logical inference is, in principle, invalid. On the other hand, nothing is more obvious than that we frequently make false inferences: from ignorance of some of the factors involved, from inattention, from inefficiencies in the system of symbols (linguistic or otherwise) which we are using, from the secret influence of our unconscious wishes or fears. We are therefore driven to combine a steadfast faith in inference as such with a wholesome scepticism about each particular instance of inference in the mind of a human thinker.

Christian Reflections

It is Reason herself which teaches us not to rely on Reason only in this matter. For Reason knows that she cannot work without materials. When it becomes clear that you cannot find out by reasoning whether the cat is in the linen-cupboard, it is Reason herself who whispers, "Go and look. This is not my job: it is a matter for the senses." So here. The materials for correcting our abstract conception of God cannot be supplied by Reason: she will be the first to tell you to go and try experience—"Oh, taste and see!" For of course she will have already pointed out that your present position is absurd. As long as we remain Erudite Limpets we are forgetting that if no-one had ever seen more of God than we, we should have no reason even to believe Him immaterial, immutable, impassible and all the rest of it. Even that negative knowledge which seems to us so enlightened is only a relic left over from the positive knowledge of better men—only the pattern which that heavenly wave left on the sand when it retreated.

Miracles

RELIGION

It is well to have specifically holy places, and things, and days, for, without these focal points or reminders, the belief that all is holy and "big with God" will soon dwindle into a mere sentiment. But if these holy places, things, and days cease to remind us, if they obliterate our awareness that all ground is holy and every bush (could we but perceive it) a Burning Bush, then the hallows begin to do harm. Hence both the necessity, and the perennial danger, of "religion."

Letters to Malcolm: Chiefly on Prayer

Of all bad men religious bad men are the worst.

Reflections on the Psalms

In the days when most people had a religion, what he meant by "an interest in religion" could hardly have existed. For of course religious people—that is, people when they are being religious— are not "interested in religion." Men who have gods worship those gods; it is the spectators who describe this as "religion." The Maenads thought about Dionysus, not about religion. Mutatis mutandis this goes for Christians too. The moment a man seriously accepts a deity his interest in "religion" is at an end. He's got something else to think about.

God in the Dock

But even in this present life, there is danger in the very concept of religion. It carries the suggestion that this is one more department of life, an extra department added to the economic, the social, the intellectual, the recreational, and all the rest. But that whose claims are infinite can have no standing as a department. Either it is an illusion or else our whole life falls under it. We have no non-religious activities; only religious and irreligious.

Letters to Malcolm: Chiefly on Prayer

I could not believe Christianity if I were forced to say that there were a thousand religions in the world of which 999 were pure nonsense and the thousandth (fortunately) true. My conversion, very largely, depended on recognizing Christianity as the completion, the actualization, the entelechy, of something that had never been wholly absent from the mind of man. And I still think that the agnostic argument from similarities between Christianity and paganism works only if you know the answer. If you start by knowing on other grounds that Christianity is false, then the pagan stories may be another nail in its coffin: just as if you started by knowing that there were no such things as crocodiles then the various stories about dragons might help to confirm your disbelief. But if the truth or falsehood of Christianity is the very question you are discussing, then the argument from anthropology is surely a petition [in logic, the fallacy of the circular argument].

God in the Dock

I thought I saw how stories of this kind [*The Chronicles of Narnia*] could steal past a certain inhibition which had paralyzed much of my own religion since childhood. Why did one find it so hard to feel as one was told one ought to feel about God or about the sufferings of Christ? I thought the chief reason was that one was told one ought to. An obligation to feel can freeze feelings. And reverence itself did harm. The whole subject was associated with lowered voices; almost as if it were something medical. But suppose by casting all these things into an imaginary world, stripping them of their stained-glass and Sunday school associations, one could make them for the first time appear in their real potency? Could one not thus steal past those watchful dragons? I thought one could.

C. S. Lewis on Stories

REPENTANCE

Christianity tells people to repent and promises them forgiveness. It therefore has nothing (as far as I know) to say to people who do not know they have done anything to repent of and who do not feel that they need any forgiveness. It is after you have realised that there is a real Moral Law, and a Power behind the law, and that you have broken that law and put yourself wrong with that Power—it is after all this, and not a moment sooner, that Christianity begins to talk.

Fallen man is not simply an imperfect creature who needs improvement: he is a rebel who must lay down his arms. Laying down your arms, surrendering, saying you are sorry, realising that you have been on the wrong track and getting ready to start life over again from the ground floor—that is the only way out of a "hole." This process of surrender—this movement full speed astern—is what Christians call repentance. Now repentance is no fun at all. It is something much harder than merely eating humble pie. It means unlearning all the self-conceit and self-will that we have been training ourselves into for thousands of years. It means killing part of yourself, undergoing a kind of death. In fact, it needs a good man to repent. And here comes the catch. Only a bad person needs to repent: only a good person can repent perfectly. The worse you are the more you need it and the less you can do it. The only person who could do it perfectly would be a perfect person—and he would not need it.

Remember, this repentance, this willing submission to humiliation and a kind of death, is not something God demands of you before He will take you back and which He could let you off if He chose: it is simply a description of what going back to Him is like. If you ask God to take you back without it, you are really asking Him to let you go back without going back. It cannot happen. Very well, then, we must go through with it. But the same badness which makes us need it makes us unable to do it. Can we do it if God helps us? Yes, but what do we mean when we talk of God helping us? We mean God putting into us a bit of Himself, so to speak. He lends us a little of His reasoning powers and that is how we think. He puts a little of His love into us and that is how we love one another. When you teach a child writing, you hold its hand while it forms the letters: that is, it forms the letters because you are forming them. We love and reason because God loves and reasons and holds our hand while we do it. Now if we had not fallen, that would be all plain sailing. But unfortunately we now need God's help in order to do something which God, in His own nature, never does at all—to surrender, to suffer, to submit, to die.

Mere Christianity

Every uncorrected error and unrepented sin is, in its own right, a fountain of fresh error and fresh sin flowing on to the end of time.

The Problem of Pain

"You had better be careful of your thoughts here," said the Guide. "Do not confuse Repentance with Disgust: for the one comes from the Landlord and the other from the Enemy."

The Pilgrim's Regress

RESURRECTION OF THE BODY

As St. Augustine said, the rapture of the saved soul will "flow over" into the glorified body. In the light of our present specialised and depraved appetites we cannot imagine this *torrens voluptatis* ["waterfall of pleasure"], and I warn everyone most seriously not to try. But it must be mentioned, to drive out thoughts even more misleading—thoughts that what is saved is a mere ghost, or that the risen body lives in numb insensibility. The body was made for the Lord, and these dismal fancies are wide of the mark.

The Weight of Glory

McPhee was arguing against the Christian doctrine of the resurrection of the human body. I was his victim at the moment and he was pressing on me in his Scots way with such questions as "So you think you're going to have guts and palate for ever in a world where there'll be no eating, and genital organs in a world without copulation? Man, ye'll have a grand time of it!" when Ransom suddenly burst out with great excitement, "Oh, don't you see, you ass, that there's a difference between a transsensuous life and a non-sensuous life?" That, of course, directed McPhee's fire to him. What emerged was that in Ransom's opinion the present functions and appetites of the body would disappear, not because they were atrophied but because they were, as he said "engulfed."

Perelandra

It is not easy to define what we mean by an "essentially human body." The records show that Our Lord's Risen Body could pass through closed doors, which human bodies can't: but also that it could eat. We shall know what a glorified body is when we have one ourselves: till then, I think we must acquiesce in mystery.

The Collected Letters of C. S. Lewis, Volume III

About the resurrection of the body. I agree with you that the old picture of the soul re-assuming the corpse—perhaps blown to bits or long since usefully dissipated through nature—is absurd. Nor is it what St. Paul's words imply. And I admit that if you ask me what I substitute for this, I have only speculations to offer.

The principle behind these speculations is this. We are not, in this doctrine, concerned with matter as such at all; with waves and atoms and all that. What the soul cries out for is the resurrection of the senses. Even in this life matter would be nothing to us if it were not the source of sensations.

Now we already have some feeble and intermittent power of raising dead sensations from their graves. I mean, of course, memory.

You see the way my thought is moving. But don't run away with the idea that when I speak of the resurrection of the body I mean merely that the blessed dead will have excellent memories of their sensuous experience on earth. I mean it the other way round: that memory as we now know it is a dim foretaste, a mirage even, of a power which the soul, or rather Christ in the soul (He went to "prepare a place" for us), will exercise hereafter. It need no longer be intermittent. Above all, it need no longer be private to the soul in which it occurs. I cannot communicate to you the fields of my boyhood—they are building-estates to-day—only imperfectly, by words. Perhaps the day is coming when I can take you for a walk through them.

At present we tend to think of the soul as somehow "inside" the body. But the glorified body of the resurrection as I conceive it—the sensuous life raised from its death—will be inside the soul. As God is not in space but space is in God.

I have slipped in "glorified" almost unawares. But this glorification is not only promised, it is already foreshadowed. The dullest of us knows how memory can transfigure; how often some momentary glimpse of beauty in boyhood

is a whisper
Which memory will warehouse as a shout.

Don't talk to me of the "illusions" of memory. Why should what we see at the moment be more "real" than what we see from ten years' distance? It is indeed an illusion to believe that the blue hills on the horizon would still look blue if you went to them. But the fact that they are blue five miles away, and the fact that they are green when you are on them, are equally good facts. Traherne's "orient and immortal wheat" or Wordsworth's landscape "apparelled in celestial light" may not have been so radiant in the past when it was present as in the remembered past. That is the beginning of the glorification. One day they will be more radiant still. Thus in the sense-bodies of the redeemed the whole New Earth will arise. The same, yet not the same, as this. It was sown in corruption, it is raised in incorruption.

I dare not omit, though it may be mocked and misunderstood, the extreme example. The strangest discovery of a widower's life is the possibility, sometimes, of recalling with detailed and uninhibited imagination, with tenderness and gratitude, a passage of carnal love, yet with no re-awakening of concupiscence. And when it occurs (it must not be sought) awe comes upon us. It is like seeing nature itself rising from its grave. What was sown in momentariness is raised in still permanence. What was sown as a becoming, rises as being. Sown in subjectivity, it rises in objectivity. The transitory secret of two is now a chord in the ultimate music.

"But this," you protest, "is no resurrection of the body. You give the dead a sort of dream world and dream bodies. They are not real." Surely neither less nor more real than those you have always known? You know better than I that the "real world" of our present experience (coloured, resonant, soft or hard, cool or warm, all corseted by perspective) has no place in the world described by physics or even by physiology. Matter enters our experience only by becoming sensation (when we perceive it) or conception (when we understand it). That is, by becoming soul. That element in the soul which it becomes will, in my view, be raised and glorified; the hills and valleys of Heaven will be to those you now experience not as a copy is to an original, nor as a substitute is to the genuine article, but as the flower to the root, or the diamond to the coal. It will be eternally true that they originated with matter; let us therefore bless matter. But in entering our soul as alone it can enter—that is, by being perceived and known—matter has turned into soul (like the Undines who acquired a soul by marriage with a mortal).

I don't say the resurrection of this body will happen at once. It may well be that this part of us sleeps in death, and the intellectual soul is sent to Lenten lands where she fasts in naked spirituality—a ghost-like and imperfectly human condition. I don't imply that an angel is a ghost. But naked spirituality is in accordance with his nature; not, I think, with ours. (A two-legged horse is maimed, but not a two-legged man.) Yet from that fast my hope is that we shall return and re-assume the wealth we have laid down.

Then the new earth and sky, the same yet not the same as these, will rise in us as we have risen in Christ. And once again, after who knows what aeons of the silence and the dark, the birds will sing and the waters flow, and lights and shadows move across the hills, and the faces of our friends laugh upon us with amazed recognition.

Guesses, of course, only guesses. If they are not true, something better will be. For "we know that we shall be made like Him, for we shall see Him as He is."

Letters to Malcolm: Chiefly on Prayer

Then Aslan stopped, and the children looked into the stream. And there, on the golden gravel of the bed of the stream, lay King Caspian, dead, with the water flowing over him like liquid glass. His long white beard swayed in it like water-weed. And all three stood and wept. Even the Lion wept: great Lion-tears, each tear more precious than the Earth would be if it was a single solid diamond. And Jill noticed that Eustace looked neither like a child crying, nor like a boy crying and wanting to hide it, but like a grown-up crying. At least, that is the nearest she could get to it; but really, as she said, people don't seem to have any particular ages on that mountain.

"Son of Adam," said Aslan, "Go into that thicket and pluck the thorn that you will find there, and bring it to me."

Eustace obeyed. The thorn was a foot long and sharp as a rapier.

"Drive it into my paw, Son of Adam," said Aslan, holding up his right fore-paw and spreading out the great pads towards Eustace.

"Must I?" said Eustace.

"Yes," said Aslan.

Then Eustace set his teeth and drove the thorn into the Lion's pad. And there came out a great drop of blood, redder than all redness that you have ever seen or imagined. And it splashed into the stream over the dead body of the King. At the same moment the doleful music stopped. And the dead King began to be changed. His white beard turned to grey, and from grey to yellow, and got shorter and vanished altogether; and his sunken cheeks grew round and fresh, and the wrinkles were smoothed, and his eyes opened, and his eyes and lips both laughed, and suddenly he leaped up and stood before them—a very young man, or a boy. (But Jill couldn't say which, because of people having no particular ages in Aslan's country. Even in this world, of course, it is the stupidest children who are most childish and the stupidest grown-ups who are most grown-up.) And he rushed to Aslan and flung his arms as far as they would go round the huge neck; and he gave Aslan the strong kisses of a King, and Aslan gave him the wild kisses of a Lion.

At last Caspian turned to the others. He gave a great laugh of astonished joy.

The Silver Chair

RICHES

Christ said it was difficult for "the rich" to enter the Kingdom of Heaven, referring, no doubt, to "riches" in the ordinary sense. But I think it really covers riches in every sense—good fortune, health, popularity, and all the things one wants to have. All these things tend—just as money tends—to make you feel independent of God, because if you have them you are happy already and contented in this life.

God in the Dock

SAINTS

God is not merely mending, not simply restoring a status quo. Redeemed humanity is to be something more glorious than unfallen humanity would have been, more glorious than any unfallen race now is (if at this moment the night sky conceals any such). The greater the sin, the greater the mercy: the deeper the death, the brighter the re-birth. And this super-added glory will, with true vicariousness, exalt all creatures, and those who have never fallen will thus bless Adam's fall.

Miracles

When Dante saw the great apostles in heaven they affected him like mountains. There's lots to be said against devotions to saints; but at least they keep on reminding us that we are very small people compared with them. How much smaller before their Master?

Letters to Malcolm: Chiefly on Prayer

SALVATION

The New Testament is always talking . . . about Christians "being born again"; it talks about them "putting on Christ"; about Christ "being formed in us"; about our coming to "have the mind of Christ.". . . [These] mean that a real Person, Christ, here and now, in that very room where you are saying your prayers, is doing things to you. It is not a question of a good man who died two thousand years ago. It is a living Man, still as much a man as you, and still as much God as He was when He created the world, really coming and interfering with your very self; killing the old natural self in you and replacing it with the kind of self He has.

Mere Christianity

The N.T. is highly paradoxical. St. Paul at the outset of an epistle sometimes talks as if the converts whom he is addressing were already wholly new creatures, already in the world of light, their old nature completely crucified. Yet by the end of the same epistle he will be warning the same people to avoid the very grossest vices.

Of himself he speaks sometimes as if his reward was perfectly sure: elsewhere he fears lest, having preached to others, he shd. be himself a castaway.

Our Lord Himself sometimes speaks as if all depended on faith, yet in the parable of the sheep and the goats all seems to depend on works: even works done or undone by those who had no idea what they were doing or undoing.

The best I can do about these mysteries is to think that the N.T. gives us a sort of double vision. *A.* Into our salvation as eternal fact, as it (and all else) is in the timeless vision of God. *B.* Into the same thing as a process worked out in time. Both must be true in some sense but it is beyond our capacity to envisage both together. Can one get a faint idea of it by thinking of *A.,* A musical score as it is written down with all the notes there at once; *B.,* The same thing played as a process in time? For practical purposes, however, it seems to me we must usually live by the second vision, "working out our own salvation in fear and trembling" (but it adds "for"—not "though"—but "for"—"it is God who worketh in us").

And in this temporal process surely God saves different souls in different ways? To preach instantaneous conversion and eternal security as if they must be the experiences of all who are saved, seems to me v. dangerous: the very way to drive some into presumption and others into despair. How v. different were the callings of the disciples.

I don't agree that if anyone were completely a new creature, you and I wd. necessarily recognise him as such. It takes holiness to detect holiness.

The Collected Letters of C. S. Lewis, Volume III

SANCTIFICATION

Die before you die. There is no chance after.

Till We Have Faces

Everyone who accepts the teaching of St. Paul must have a belief in "sanctification." But I should, myself, be v. chary of describing such operations of the Holy Ghost as "experiences" if by experiences we mean things necessarily discoverable by introspection. And I should be still more chary of mapping out a series of such experiences as an indispensable norm (or syllabus!) for all Christians. I think the ways in which God saves us are probably infinitely various and admit varying degrees of consciousness in the patient. Anything wh. sets him saying "Now . . . Stage II ought to be coming along . . . is this it?" I think bad and likely to lead some to presumption and others to despair. We must leave God to dress the wound and not keep on taking peeps under the bandage for ourselves.

I take it that what St. Paul means by Sanctification is the process of "Christ being formed in us," the process of becoming like Christ—so that the title of the medieval book (wh. I hope you read) *The Imitation of Christ* is a formula for the Christian life. And no doubt sanctification wd. be the correction both of our congenital or original sinfulness and of our actual particular sins. I haven't seen that the distinction is v. important, since the latter are the expression of the former.

The Collected Letters of C. S. Lewis, Volume II

"Say what you like," we shall be told, "the apocalyptic beliefs of the first Christians have been proved to be false. It is clear from the New Testament that they all expected the Second Coming in their own lifetime. And, worse still, they had a reason, and one which you will find very embarrassing. Their Master had told them so. He shared, and indeed created, their delusion. He said in so many words, 'this generation shall not pass till all these things be done.' And he was wrong. He clearly knew no more about the end of the world than anyone else.". . .

It is certainly the most embarrassing verse in the Bible. Yet how teasing, also, that within fourteen words of it should come the statement "But of that day and that hour knoweth no man, no, not the angels which are in heaven, neither the Son, but the Father." The one exhibition of error and the one confession of ignorance grow side by side. That they stood thus in the mouth of Jesus Himself, and were not merely placed thus by the reporter, we surely need not doubt. Unless the reporter were perfectly honest he would never have recorded the confession of ignorance at all; he could have had no motive for doing so except a desire to tell the whole truth. And unless later copyists were equally honest they would never have preserved the (apparently) mistaken prediction about "this generation" after the passage of time had shown the (apparent) mistake. . . .

The idea which here shuts out the Second Coming from our minds, the idea of the world slowly ripening to perfection, is a myth, not a generalization from experience. And it is a myth which distracts us from our real duties and our real interest. It is our attempt to guess the plot of a drama in which we are the characters. But how can the characters in a play guess the plot? We are not the playwright, we are not the producer, we are not even the audience. We are on the stage. To play well the scenes in which we are "on" concerns us much more than to guess about the scenes that follow it. . . .

The doctrine of the Second Coming teaches us that we do not and cannot know when the world drama will end. The curtain may be rung down at any moment: say, before you have finished reading this paragraph. This seems to some people intolerably frustrating. So many things would be interrupted. Perhaps you were going to get married next month, perhaps you were going to get a raise next week: you may be on the verge of a great scientific discovery; you may be maturing great social and political reforms. Surely no good and wise God would be so very unreasonable as to cut all this short? Not now, of all moments! . . .

The doctrine of the Second Coming, then, is not to be rejected because it conflicts with our favorite modern mythology. It is, for that very reason, to be the more valued and made more frequently the subject of meditation. It is the medicine our condition especially needs.

What death is to each man, the Second Coming is to the whole human race. We all believe, I suppose, that a man should "sit loose" to his own individual life, should remember how short, precarious, temporary, and provisional a thing it is; should never give all his heart to anything which will end when his life ends.

What modern Christians find it harder to remember is that the whole life of humanity in this world is also precarious, temporary, provisional.

The World's Last Night

SEEKING GOD

Looking for God—or Heaven—by exploring space is like reading or seeing all Shakespeare's plays in the hope that you will find Shakespeare as one of the characters.

I never had the experience of looking for God. It was the other way round; He was the hunter (or so it seemed to me) and I was the deer. He stalked me like a redskin, took unerring aim, and fired. And I am very thankful that that is how the first (conscious) meeting occurred. It forearms one against subsequent fears that the whole thing was only wish fulfilment. Something one didn't wish for can hardly be that.

Christian Reflections

Amiable agnostics will talk cheerfully about "man's search for God." To me, as I then was, they might as well have talked about the mouse's search for the cat.

Surprised by Joy

SELF

Since I have begun to pray, I find my extreme view of personality changing. My own empirical self is becoming more important, and this is exactly the opposite of self-love. You don't teach a seed how to die into treehood by throwing it into the fire: and it has to become a good seed before it's worth burying.

The Collected Letters of C. S. Lewis, Volume II

In this height and depth and breadth the little idea of herself which [Jane Studdock] had hitherto called me dropped down and vanished, unfluttering, into bottomless distance, like a bird in a space without air. The name "me" was the name of a being whose existence she had never suspected, a being that did not yet fully exist but which was demanded. It was a person (not the person she had thought), yet also a thing, a made thing, made to please Another and in Him to please all others, a thing being made at this very moment, without its choice, in a shape it had never dreamed of. And the making went on amidst a kind of splendour or sorrow or both, whereof she could not tell whether it was in the moulding hands or in the kneaded lump.

That Hideous Strength

When the time comes to you at which you will be forced at last to utter the speech which has lain at the center of your soul for years, which you have, all that time, idiot-like, been saying over and over, you'll not talk about joy of words. I saw well why the gods do not speak to us openly, nor let us answer. Till that word can be dug out of us, why should they hear the babble that we think we mean? How can they meet us face to face till we have faces?

Till We Have Faces

The terrible thing, the almost impossible thing, is to hand over your whole self—all your wishes and precautions—to Christ.

Until you have given up your self to Him you will not have a real self.

Mere Christianity

We therefore agree with Aristotle that what is intrinsically right may well be agreeable, and that the better a man is the more he will like it; but we agree with Kant so far as to say that there is one right act—that of self-surrender—which cannot be willed to the height by fallen creatures unless it is unpleasant. And we must add that this one right act includes all other righteousness, and that the supreme cancelling of Adam's fall, the movement "full speed astern" by which we retrace our long journey from Paradise, the untying of the old, hard knot, must be when the creature, with no desire to aid it, stripped naked to the bare willing of obedience, embraces what is contrary to its nature, and does that for which only one motive is possible.

The Problem of Pain

A rejection, or in Scripture's strong language, a crucifixion of the natural self is the passport to everlasting life. Nothing that has not died will be resurrected.

The Weight of Glory

Every natural love will rise again and live forever in this country: but none will rise again until it has been buried.

The Great Divorce

The more we get what we now call "ourselves" out of the way and let Him take us over, the more truly ourselves we become.... I am not, in my natural state, nearly so much of a person as I like to believe: most of what I call "me" can be very easily explained. It is when I turn to Christ, when I give myself up to His Personality, that I first begin to have a real personality of my own.

Mere Christianity

SELF-CENTEREDNESS

The natural life in each of us is something self-centred, something that wants to be petted and admired, to take advantage of other lives, to exploit the whole universe. . . . [The natural life] knows that if the spiritual life gets hold of it, all its self-centredness and self-will are going to be killed and it is ready to fight tooth and nail to avoid that.

Mere Christianity

AS THE RUIN FALLS

All this is flashy rhetoric about loving you.
I never had a selfless thought since I was born.
I am mercenary and self-seeking through and through:
I want God, you, all friends, merely to serve my turn.

Peace, re-assurance, pleasure, are the goals I seek,
I cannot crawl one inch outside my proper skin:
I talk of love—a scholar's parrot may talk Greek—
But self-imprisoned, always end where I begin.

Only that now you have taught me (but how late) my lack.
I see the chasm. And everything you are was making

My heart into a bridge by which I might get back
From exile, and grow man. And now the bridge is breaking.

For this I bless you as the ruin falls. The pains
You give me are more precious than all other gains.

The Collected Poems of C. S. Lewis

SELF-CONSCIOUSNESS

We should, I believe, distrust states of mind which turn our attention upon ourselves. Even at our sins we should look no longer than is necessary to know and to repent them: and our virtues or progress (if any) are certainly a dangerous object of contemplation. When the sun is vertically above a man he casts no shadow: similarly when we have come to the Divine meridian our spiritual shadow (that is, our consciousness of self) will vanish. One will thus in a sense be almost nothing: a room to be filled by God and our blessed fellow creatures, who in their turn are rooms we help to fill. But how far one is from this at present!

The Collected Letters of C. S. Lewis, Volume III

SELF-ESTEEM

I would prefer to combat the "I'm special" feeling not by the thought "I'm no more special than anyone else," but by the feeling "Everyone is as special as me." In one way there is no difference, I grant, for both remove the speciality. But there is a difference in another way. The first might lead you to think, "I'm only one of the crowd like everyone else." But the second leads to the truth that there isn't any crowd. No one is like anyone else. All are "members" (organs) in the Body of Christ. All different and all necessary to the whole and to one another; each loved by God individually, as if it were the only creature in existence.

The Collected Letters of C. S. Lewis, Volume III

"And join in I hope, Sir!" added the largest of the centaurs.

"And now! Those who can't keep up—that is, children, dwarfs, and small animals—must ride on the backs of those who can—that is, lions, centaurs, unicorns, horses, giants and eagles. Those who are good with their noses must come in the front with us lions to smell out where the battle is. Look lively and sort yourselves."

And with a great deal of bustle and cheering they did. The most pleased of the lot was the other lion, who kept running about everywhere pretending to be very busy but really in order to say to everyone he met, "Did you hear what he said? Us lions. That means him and me. Us lions. That's what I like about Aslan. No side, no stand-off-ishness. Us lions. That meant him and me."

At least he went on saying this till Aslan had loaded him up with three dwarfs, one Dryad, two rabbits, and a hedgehog. That steadied him a bit.

The Lion, the Witch and the Wardrobe

Humility disarms us, and we seldom acknowledge a man's moral superiority to us in guilelessness and truth without reimbursing our self-esteem by a feeling that we are at least equally superior to him in acuteness and knowledge of the world.

Studies in Words

[The demon Screwtape writes:] [God, the "Enemy,"] wants to kill their animal self-love as soon as possible; but it is His long-term policy, I fear, to restore to them a new kind of self-love, charity and gratitude for all selves, including their own; when they have really learned to love their neighbours as themselves, they will be allowed to love themselves as their neighbours.

The Screwtape Letters

SELF-SUFFICIENCY

They [Adam and Eve] wanted, as we say, to "call their souls their own." But that means to live a lie, for our souls are not, in fact, our own. They wanted some corner in the universe of which they could say to God, "This is our business, not yours." But there is no such corner. They wanted to be nouns, but they were, and eternally must be, mere adjectives.

The Problem of Pain

"This is Caspian, Sir," he said.

And Caspian knelt and kissed the Lion's paw.

"Welcome, Prince," said Aslan. "Do you feel yourself sufficient to take up the Kingship of Narnia?"

"I—I don't think I do, Sir," said Caspian. "I'm only a kid."

"Good," said Aslan. "If you had felt yourself sufficient, it would have been a proof that you were not. Therefore, under us and under the High King, you shall be King of Narnia, Lord of Cair Paravel and Emperor of the Lone Islands. You and your heirs while your race lasts."

Prince Caspian

SELF-UNDERSTANDING

Be sure that the ins and outs of your individuality are no mystery to Him; and one day they will no longer be a mystery to you.

The Problem of Pain

I sometimes pray not for self-knowledge in general but for just so much self-knowledge at the moment as I can bear and use at the moment; the little daily dose.

Have we any reason to suppose that total self-knowledge, if it were given us, would be for our good? Children and fools, we are told, should never look at half-done work; and we are not yet, I trust, even half-done.

Letters to Malcolm: Chiefly on Prayer

SERVICE

You may put out of your head any idea of "not having a claim" on any help I can give. Every human being, still more every Christian, has an absolute claim on me for any service I can render them without neglecting other duties.

The Collected Letters of C. S. Lewis, Volume II

SILENCE

[The demon Screwtape writes:] Music and silence—how I detest them both! How thankful we should be that ever since our Father entered Hell—though longer ago than humans, reckoning in light years, could express—no square inch of infernal space and no moment of infernal time has been surrendered to either of those abominable forces, but all has been occupied by Noise— Noise, the grand dynamism, the audible expression of all that is exultant, ruthless, and virile—Noise which alone defends us from silly qualms, despairing scruples, and impossible desires. We will make the whole universe a noise in the end. We have already made great strides in this direction as regards the Earth. The melodies and silences of Heaven will be shouted down in the end. But I admit we are not yet loud enough, or anything like it.

The Screwtape Letters

We may find a violence in some of the traditional imagery which tends to obscure the changelessness of God, the peace, which nearly all who approach Him have reported—the "still, small voice." And it is here, I think, that the pre-Christian imagery is least suggestive. Yet even here, there is a danger lest the half con- scious picture of some huge thing at rest—a clear, still ocean, a dome of "white radiance"—should smuggle in ideas of inertia or vacuity. The stillness in which the mystics approach Him is intent and alert—at the opposite pole from sleep or reverie. They are becoming like Him. Silences in the physical world occur in empty places: but the ultimate Peace is silent through very density of life. Saying is swallowed up in being. There is no movement because His action (which is Himself) is timeless.

Miracles

SIN

The sins of the flesh are bad, but they are the least bad of all sins. All the worst pleasures are purely spiritual: the pleasure of putting other people in the wrong, of bossing and patronising and spoiling sport, and back-biting; the pleasures of power, of hatred. For there are two things inside me, competing with the human self which I must try to become. They are the Animal self, and the Diabolical self. The Diabolical self is the worst of the two. That is why a cold, self-righteous prig who goes regularly to church may be far nearer to hell than a prostitute. But, of course, it is better to be neither.

Mere Christianity

When I said that your besetting sin was Indolence and mine Pride I was thinking of the old classification of the seven deadly sins: They are *Gula* (Gluttony), *Luxuria* (Unchastity), *Accidia* (Indolence), *Ira* (Anger), *Superbia* (Pride), *Invidia* (Envy), *Avaricia* (Avarice). *Accidia*, which is sometimes called *Tristicia* (despondence), is the kind of indolence which comes from indifference to the good—the mood in which though it tries to play on us we have no string to respond. *Pride*, on the other hand, is the mother of *all* sins, and the original sin of Lucifer—so you are rather better off than I am. You at your worst are an instrument unstrung: I am an instrument strung but preferring to play itself because it thinks it knows the tune better than the Musician.

The Collected Letters of C. S. Lewis, Volume I

DEADLY SINS

> *Through our lives thy meshes run*
> *Deft as spiders' catenation,*
> *Crossed and crossed again and spun*
> *Finer than the fiend's temptation.*
>
> *Greed into herself would turn*
> *All that's sweet: but let her follow*
> *Still that path, and greed will learn*
> *How the whole world is hers to swallow.*
>
> *Sloth that would find out a bed*
> *Blind to morning, deaf to waking,*
> *Shuffling shall at last be led*
> *To the peace that knows no breaking.*
>
> *Lechery, that feels sharp lust*
> *Sharper from each promised staying,*
> *Goes at long last—go she must—*
> *Where alone is sure allaying.*
>
> *Anger, postulating still*
> *Inexcusables to shatter,*
> *From the shelter of thy will*
> *Finds herself her proper matter.*
>
> *Envy had rather die than see*
> *Other's course her own outflying;*
> *She will pay with death to be*
> *Where her Best brooks no denying.*

Pride, that from each step, anew
Mounts again with mad aspiring,
Must find all at last, save you,
Set too low for her desiring.

Avarice, while she finds an end,
Counts but small the largest treasure.
Whimperingly at last she'll bend
To take free what has no measure.

So inexorably thou
On thy shattered foes pursuing,
Never a respite dost allow
Save what works their own undoing.

The Collected Poems of C. S. Lewis

Every sin is the distortion of an energy breathed into us—an energy which, if not thus distorted, would have blossomed into one of those holy acts whereof "God did it" and "I did it" are both true descriptions. We poison the wine as He decants it into us; murder a melody He would play with us as the instrument. We caricature the self-portrait He would paint. Hence all sin, whatever else it is, is sacrilege.

Letters to Malcolm: Chiefly on Prayer

[The demon Screwtape writes:] Even of his sins the Enemy does not want him to think too much: once they are repented, the sooner the man turns his attention outward, the better the Enemy is pleased.

The Screwtape Letters

SPIRITUAL LIFE

But what man, in his natural condition, has not got, is Spiritual life—the higher and different sort of life that exists in God. We use the same word life for both: but if you thought that both must therefore be the same sort of thing, that would be like thinking that the "greatness" of space and the "greatness" of God were the same sort of greatness. In reality, the difference between Biological life and Spiritual life is so important that I am going to give them two distinct names. The Biological sort, which comes to us through Nature, and which (like everything else in Nature) is always tending to run down and decay so that it can only be kept up by incessant subsidies from Nature in the form of air, water, food, etc., is *Bios*. The Spiritual life, which is in God from all eternity, and which made the whole natural universe, is *Zoe*. *Bios* has, to be sure, a certain shadowy or symbolic resemblance to *Zoe*: but only the sort of resemblance there is between a photo and a place, or a statue and a man. A man who changed from having *Bios* to having *Zoe* would have gone through as big a change as a statue which changed from being a carved stone to being a real man.

Mere Christianity

TEMPTATION

[The demon Screwtape writes:] In the first place I have always found that the Trough periods of the human undulation provide excellent opportunity for all sensual temptations, particularly those of sex. This may surprise you, because, of course, there is more physical energy, and therefore more potential appetite, at the Peak periods; but you must remember that the powers of resistance are then also at their highest. The health and spirits which you want to use in producing lust can also, alas, be very easily used for work or play or thought or innocuous merriment. The attack has a much better chance of success when the man's whole inner world is drab and cold and empty. And it is also to be noted that the Trough sexuality is subtly different in quality from that of the Peak—much less likely to lead to the milk-and-water phenomenon which the humans call "being in love," much more easily drawn into perversions, much less contaminated by those generous and imaginative and even spiritual concomitants which often render human sexuality so disappointing. It is the same with other desires of the flesh. You are much more likely to make your man a sound drunkard by pressing drink on him as an anodyne when he is dull and weary than by encouraging him to use it as a means of merriment among his friends when he is happy and expansive. Never forget that when we are dealing with any pleasure in its healthy and normal and satisfying form, we are, in a sense, on the Enemy's ground. I know we have won many a soul through pleasure. All the same, it is His invention, not ours.

He made the pleasures: all our research so far has not enabled us to produce one. All we can do is to encourage the humans to take the pleasures which our Enemy has produced, at times, or in ways, or in degrees, which He has forbidden. Hence we always try to work away from the natural condition of any pleasure to that in which it is least natural, least redolent of its Maker, and least pleasurable. An ever increasing craving for an ever diminishing pleasure is the formula. It is more certain; and it's better style. To get the man's soul and give him nothing in return—that is what really gladdens Our Father's heart. And the troughs are the time for beginning the process.

The Screwtape Letters

This was the first thing Mark had been asked to do which he himself, before he did it, clearly knew to be criminal. But the moment of his consent almost escaped his notice; certainly, there was no struggle, no sense of turning a corner. There may have been a time in the world's history when such moments fully revealed their gravity, with witches prophesying on a blasted heath or visible Rubicons to be crossed. But, for him, it all slipped past in a chatter of laughter, of that intimate laughter between fellow professionals, which of all earthly powers is strongest to make men do very bad things before they are yet, individually, very bad men.

The Hideous Strength

We never find out the strength of the evil impulse inside us until we try to fight it: and Christ, because He was the only man who never yielded to temptation, is also the only man who knows to the full what temptation means—the only complete realist.

Mere Christianity

[The demon Screwtape writes:] The most alarming thing in your last account of the patient is that he is making none of those confident resolutions which marked his original conversion. No more lavish promises of perpetual virtue, I gather; not even the expectation of an endowment of "grace" for life, but only a hope for the daily and hourly pittance to meet the daily and hourly temptation! This is very bad.

The Screwtape Letters

TIME

Our life comes to us moment by moment. One moment disappears before the next comes along: and there is room for very little in each. That is what Time is like. And of course you and I tend to take it for granted that this Time series—this arrangement of past, present and future—is not simply the way life comes to us but the way all things really exist. We tend to assume that the whole universe and God Himself are always moving on from past to future just as we do. But many learned men do not agree with that. It was the Theologians who first started the idea that some things are not in Time at all: later the Philosophers took it over: and now some of the scientists are doing the same.

Almost certainly God is not in Time. His life does not consist of moments following one another. If a million people are praying to Him at ten-thirty tonight, He need not listen to them all in that one little snippet which we call ten-thirty. Ten-thirty—and every other moment from the beginning of the world—is always the Present for Him. If you like to put it that way, He has all eternity in which to listen to the split second of prayer put up by a pilot as his plane crashes in flames. . . .

If you picture Time as a straight line along which we have to travel, then you must picture God as the whole page on which the line is drawn. We come to the parts of the line one by one: we have to leave A behind before we get to B, and cannot reach C until we leave B behind. God, from above or outside or all round, contains the whole line, and sees it all.

Mere Christianity

[The demon Screwtape writes:] The humans live in time but our Enemy destines them to eternity. He therefore, I believe, wants them to attend chiefly to two things, to eternity itself, and to that point of time which they call the Present. For the Present is the point at which time touches eternity. Of the present moment, and of it only, humans have an experience analogous to the experience which our Enemy has of reality as a whole; in it alone freedom and actuality are offered them. He would therefore have them continually concerned either with eternity (which means being concerned with Him) or with the Present—either meditating on their eternal union with, or separation from, Himself, or else obeying the present voice of conscience, bearing the present cross, receiving the present grace, giving thanks for the present pleasure.

Our business is to get them away from the eternal, and from the Present. With this in view, we sometimes tempt a human (say a widow or a scholar) to live in the Past. But this is of limited value, for they have some real knowledge of the past and it has a determinate nature and, to that extent, resembles eternity. It is far better to make them live in the Future. Biological necessity makes all their passions point in that direction already, so that thought about the Future inflames hope and fear. Also, it is unknown to them, so that in making them think about it we make them think of unrealities. In a word, the Future is, of all things, the thing least like eternity. It is the most completely temporal part of time—for the Past is frozen and no longer flows, and the Present is all lit up with eternal rays.

The Screwtape Letters

I feel—can you work it out for me and tell me if it is more than a feeling?—that to make the life of the blessed dead strictly timeless is inconsistent with the resurrection of the body.

Letters to Malcolm: Chiefly on Prayer

TRINITY

At this point we must remind ourselves that Christian theology does not believe God to be a person. It believes Him to be such that in Him a trinity of persons is consistent with a unity of Deity. In that sense it believes Him to be something very different from a person, just as a cube, in which six squares are consistent with unity of the body, is different from a square. (Flatlanders, attempting to imagine a cube, would either imagine the six squares coinciding, and thus destroy their distinctness, or else imagine them set out side by side, and thus destroy the unity. Our difficulties about the Trinity are much of the same kind.)

Christian Reflections

In Christianity God is not a static thing—not even a person—but a dynamic, pulsating activity, a life, almost a kind of drama. Almost, if you will not think me irreverent, a kind of dance. The union between the Father and Son is such a live concrete thing that this union itself is a Person. . . . What grows out of the joint life of the Father and Son is a real Person, is, in fact, the Third of the three Persons who are God. . . . The whole dance, or drama, a pattern of this three-Personal life is to be played out in each one of us or (putting it the other way round) each one of us has got to enter that pattern, take his place in that dance.

Mere Christianity

"Who *are* you?" asked Shasta.

"Myself," said the Voice, very deep and low so that the earth shook: and again "Myself," loud and clear and gay: and then the third time "Myself," whispered so softly you could hardly hear it, and yet it seemed to come from all round you as if the leaves rustled with it.

Shasta was no longer afraid that the Voice belonged to something that would eat him, nor that it was the voice of a ghost. But a new and different sort of trembling came over him. Yet he felt glad too.

The Horse and His Boy

TRUST

Relying on God has to begin all over again every day as if nothing had yet been done.

The Collected Letters of C. S. Lewis, Volume II

TRUTH

"I suppose there are two views about everything," said Mark.

"Eh? Two views? There are a dozen views about everything until you know the answer. Then there's never more than one."

That Hideous Strength

[The demon Screwtape writes:] Your man has been accustomed, ever since he was a boy, to have a dozen incompatible philosophies dancing about together inside his head. He doesn't think of doctrines as primarily "true" or "false," but as "academic" or "practical," "outworn" or "contemporary," "conventional" or "ruthless." Jargon, not argument, is your best ally in keeping him from the Church. Don't waste time trying to make him think that materialism is true! Make him think it is strong, or stark, or courageous—that it is the philosophy of the future. That's the sort of thing he cares about.

The Screwtape Letters

One of the great difficulties is to keep before the audience's mind the question of Truth. They always think you are recommending Christianity not because it is true but because it is good. And in the discussion they will at every moment try to escape from the issue "True—or False" into stuff about a good society, or morals, or the incomes of Bishops, or the Spanish Inquisition, or France, or Poland—or anything whatever. You have to keep forcing them back, and again back, to the real point.

God in the Dock

You sometimes hear people say, "Religion doesn't appeal to me," and I once knew a girl who said, "Religion's all right provided it doesn't go too far." People who talk that way think religion is a thing like football or music which may suit some of us and not others, or which you may be interested in up to a point and no further. The first step towards being grown up is to realise that this is balderdash. Christianity isn't a hobby, or even a patent medicine. It makes statements: God exists—man is broken—God became a man—that man can mend all other men—no one else can—those who are not mended go into the dustbin. If these statements are true, they concern everyone, and are of infinite importance. Either zero—or infinity. Either this wire is not a live wire or else it carries a current of infinite voltage. Christianity can't be moderately important.

In Our Tongues

UNIVERSALISM

Perhaps most remarkable of all is the function—a low and primitive, yet often indispensable function—which [George MacDonald] allows to Fear in the spiritual life. . . . Reaction against early teachings might on this point have very easily driven him into a shallow liberalism. But it does not. He hopes, indeed, that all men will be saved; but that is because he hopes that all will repent. He knows (none better) that even omnipotence cannot save the unconverted. He never trifles with eternal impossibilities.

George MacDonald: An Anthology

[The fictional George MacDonald is speaking.] "Either the day must come when joy prevails and all the makers of misery are no longer able to infect it; or else for ever and ever the makers of misery can destroy in others the happiness they reject for themselves. I know it has a grand sound to say ye'll accept no salvation which leaves even one creature in the dark outside. But watch that sophistry or ye'll make a Dog in a Manger the tyrant of the universe."

The Great Divorce

"Aslan," said Lucy through her tears, "could you—will you—do something for these poor Dwarfs?"

"Dearest," said Aslan, "I will show you both what I can, and what I cannot, do." He came close to the Dwarfs and gave a low growl: low, but it set all the air shaking. But the Dwarfs said to one another, "Hear that? That's the gang at the other end of the stable. Trying to frighten us. They do it with a machine of some kind. Don't take any notice. They won't take us in again!"

Aslan raised his head and shook his mane. Instantly a glorious feast appeared on the Dwarfs' knees: pies and tongues and pigeons and trifles and ices, and each Dwarf had a goblet of good wine in his right hand. But it wasn't much use. They began eating and drinking greedily enough, but it was clear that they couldn't taste it properly. They thought they were eating and drinking only the sort of things you might find in a stable. One said he was trying to eat hay and another said he had a bit of an old turnip and a third said he'd found a raw cabbage leaf. And they raised golden goblets of rich red wine to their lips and said "Ugh! Fancy drinking dirty water out of a trough that a donkey's been at! Never thought we'd come to this." But very soon every Dwarf began suspecting that every other Dwarf had found something nicer than he had, and they started grabbing and snatching, and went on to quarrelling, till in a few minutes there was a free fight and all the good food was smeared on their faces and clothes or trodden under foot. But when at last they sat down to nurse their black eyes and their bleeding noses, they all said:

"Well, at any rate there's no Humbug here. We haven't let anyone take us in. The Dwarfs are for the Dwarfs."

"You see," said Aslan. "They will not let us help them. They have chosen cunning instead of belief. Their prison is only in their own minds, yet they are in that prison; and so afraid of being taken in that they cannot be taken out."

The Last Battle

Of course it should be pointed out that, though all salvation is through Jesus, we need not conclude that He cannot save those who have not explicitly accepted Him in this life. And it should (at least in my judgement) be made clear that we are not pronouncing all other religions to be totally false, but rather saying that in Christ whatever is true in all religions is consummated and perfected. But, on the other hand, I think we must attack wherever we meet it the nonsensical idea that mutually exclusive propositions about God can both be true.

God in the Dock

[Emeth said,] "So I went over much grass and many flowers and among all kinds of wholesome and delectable trees till lo! in a narrow place between two rocks there came to meet me a great Lion. The speed of him was like the ostrich, and his size was an elephant's; his hair was like pure gold and the brightness of his eyes like gold that is liquid in the furnace. He was more terrible than the Flaming Mountain of Lagour, and in beauty he surpassed all that is in the world even as the rose in bloom surpasses the dust of the desert. Then I fell at his feet and thought, Surely this is the hour of death, for the Lion (who is worthy of all honour) will know that I have served Tash all my days and not him. Nevertheless, it is better to see the Lion and die than to be Tisroc of the world and live and not to have seen him. But the Glorious One bent down his golden head and touched my forehead with his tongue and said, Son, thou art welcome. But I said, Alas, Lord, I am no son of thine but the servant of Tash. He answered, Child, all the service thou hast done to Tash, I account as service done to me. Then by reasons of my great desire for wisdom and understanding, I overcame my fear and questioned the Glorious One and said, Lord, is it then true, as the Ape said, that thou and Tash are one? The Lion growled so that the earth shook (but his wrath was not against me) and said, It is false. Not because he and I are one, but because we are opposites, I take to me the services which thou hast done to him. For I and he are of such different kinds that no service which is vile can be done to me, and none which is not vile can be done to him. Therefore if any man swear by Tash and keep his oath for the oath's sake, it is by me that he has truly sworn, though he know it not, and it is I who reward him. And if any man do a cruelty in my name, then, though he says the name Aslan, it is Tash whom he serves and by Tash his deed is accepted. Dost thou understand, Child? I said, Lord, thou knowest how much I understand. But I said also (for the truth constrained me), Yet I have been seeking Tash all my days. Beloved, said the Glorious One, unless thy desire had been for me thou wouldst not have sought so long and so truly. For all find what they truly seek.

"Then he breathed upon me and took away the trembling from my limbs and caused me to stand upon my feet. And after that, he said not much, but that we should meet again, and I must go further up and further in. Then he turned him about in a storm and flurry of gold and was gone suddenly.

"And since then, O Kings and Ladies, I have been wandering to find him and my happiness is so great that it even weakens me like a wound."

The Last Battle

Is it not frightfully unfair that this new life should be confined to people who have heard of Christ and been able to believe in Him? But the truth is God has not told us what His arrangements about the other people are. We do know that no man can be saved except through Christ; we do not know that only those who know Him can be saved through Him. But in the meantime, if you are worried about the people outside, the most unreasonable thing you can do is to remain outside yourself. Christians are Christ's body, the organism through which He works. Every addition to that body enables Him to do more. If you want to help those outside you must add your own little cell to the body of Christ who alone can help them. Cutting off a man's fingers would be an odd way of getting him to do more work.

Mere Christianity

On the heathen, see I Tim. IV. 10. Also in Matt. XXV. 31–46 the people don't sound as if they were believers. Also the doctrine of Christ's descending into Hell and preaching to the dead: wd. that would be outside time, and include those who died long after Him as well as those who died before He was born as Man. I don't think we know the details; we must just stick to the view that (a) all justice and mercy will be done, (b) but nevertheless it is our duty to do all we can to convert unbelievers.

I think that every prayer which is sincerely made even to a false god or to a v. imperfectly conceived true God, is accepted by the true God and that Christ saves many who do not think they know Him. For He is (dimly) present in the good side of the inferior teachers they follow. In the parable of the Sheep & Goats

(Matt. XXV. 31 and following) those who are saved do not seem to know that they have served Christ. But of course our anxiety about unbelievers is most usefully employed when it leads us not to speculation but to earnest prayer for them and the attempt to be in our own lives such good advertisements for Christianity as will make it attractive.

The Collected Letters of C. S. Lewis, Volume III

VALUES

Let us get two propositions written into our minds with indelible ink.

1) The human mind has no more power of inventing a new value than of planting a new sun in the sky or a new primary colour in the spectrum.

2) Every attempt to do so consists in arbitrarily selecting some one maxim of traditional morality, isolating it from the rest, and erecting it into an *unum necessarium* ["the one necessary thing"].

Christian Reflections

VOCATION

A vocation is a terrible thing. To be called out of nature into the supernatural life is at first (or perhaps not quite at first—the wrench of the parting may be felt later) a costly honour. Even to be called from one natural level to another is loss as well as gain. Man has difficulties and sorrows which the other primates escape. But to be called up higher still costs still more. "Get thee out of thy country, and from thy kindred, and from thy father's house," said God to Abraham (Genesis 12, 1). It is a terrible command; turn your back on all you know.

Reflections on the Psalms

It may be a given man's vocation to approach God mystically because he has the mystical faculty, but only in the same way as it is another man's duty to serve God by driving a plough because he is a good ploughman. And if anyone tried to impose mysticism as the norm of Christian life I suspect he would be making the same mistake as one who said we ought all to be fishermen because some of the apostles were.

The Collected Letters of C. S. Lewis, Volume II

We shall try, if we get the chance, to earn our living by doing well what would be worth doing even if we had not our living to earn. A considerable mortification of our avarice may be necessary. It is usually the insane jobs that lead to big money; they are often also the least laborious.

For He seems to do nothing of Himself which He can possibly delegate to His creatures. He commands us to do slowly and blunderingly what He could do perfectly and in the twinkling of an eye.

The World's Last Night

I prefer to make no judgment concerning a writer's direct "illumination" by the Holy Spirit. I have no way of knowing whether what is written is from heaven or not. I do believe that God is the Father of lights—natural lights as well as spiritual lights (James i. 17). That is, God is not interested only in Christian writers as such. He is concerned with all kinds of writing. In the same way a sacred calling is not limited to ecclesiastical functions. The man who is weeding a field of turnips is also serving God.

God in the Dock

WAR

My memories of the last war haunted my dreams for years. Military service, to be plain, includes the threat of every temporal evil: pain and death wh. is what we fear from sickness: isolation from those we love wh. is what we fear from exile: toil under arbitrary masters, injustice and humiliation, wh. is what we fear from slavery: hunger, thirst, cold and exposure wh. is what we fear from poverty. I'm not a pacifist. If it's got to be, it's got to be. But the flesh is weak and selfish and I think death wd. be much better than to live through another war.

The Collected Letters of C. S. Lewis, Volume II

I believe our cause to be, as human causes go, very righteous, and I therefore believe it to be a duty to participate in this war. And every duty is a religious duty, and our obligation to perform every duty is therefore absolute. Thus we may have a duty to rescue a drowning man, and perhaps, if we live on a dangerous coast, to learn life-saving so as to be ready for any drowning man when he turns up. It may be our duty to lose our own lives in saving him. But if anyone devoted himself to life-saving in the sense of giving it his total attention—so that he thought and spoke of nothing else and demanded the cessation of all other human activities until everyone had learned to swim—he would be a monomaniac. The rescue of drowning men is, then, a duty worth dying for, but not worth living for. It seems to me that all political duties (among which I include military duties) are of this kind. A man may have to die for our country: but no man must, in any exclusive sense, live for his country. He who surrenders himself without reservation to the temporal claims of a nation, or a party, or a class is rendering to Caesar that which, of all things, most emphatically belongs to God: himself.

The Weight of Glory

What the wars and the weather (are we in for another of those periodic ice ages?) and the atomic bomb have really done is to remind us forcibly of the sort of world we are living in and which, during the prosperous period before 1914, we were beginning to forget. And this reminder is, so far as it goes, a good thing. We have been waked from a pretty dream, and now we can begin to talk about realities.

Present Concerns

WORLD

I believe that there are many accommodating preachers, and too many practitioners in the church who are not believers. Jesus Christ did not say "Go into all the world and tell the world that it is quite right." The Gospel is something completely different. In fact, it is directly opposed to the world.

God in the Dock

The difference between us is that the Professor sees the "World" purely in terms of those threats and those allurements which depend on money. I do not. The most "worldly" society I have ever lived in is that of schoolboys: most worldly in the cruelty and arrogance of the strong, the toadyism and mutual treachery of the weak, and the unqualified snobbery of both. Nothing was so base that most members of the school proletariat would not do it, or suffer it, to win the favour of the school aristocracy: hardly any injustice too bad for the aristocracy to practice. But the class system did not in the least depend on the amount of anyone's pocket money. Who needs to care about money if most of the things he wants will be offered by cringing servility and the remainder can be taken by force.

C. S. Lewis on Stories

WORLDLINESS

A. There are two meanings of World in N.T. (i) In "God so loved the World" it means the Creation—stars, trees, beasts, men, and angels. (ii) In "Love not the World" it means the "worldly" life, i.e., the life built up by men in disregard of God, the life of money-making, ambition, snobbery, social success and "greatness."

B. Most spiritual writers distinguish two vocations for Christians (i) The monastic or contemplative life. (ii) The secular or active life. All Christians are called to abandon the "World" (sense ii) in spirit, i.e., to reject as strongly as they possibly can its standards, motives, and prizes. But some are called to "come out of it" as far as possible by renouncing private property, marriage, their professions, etc.: others have to remain "in it" but not "of it."

I of course am in the second class and write for those who are also in it. This isn't to say that I may not be (you may be sure I am) far too much "of it." You, and your friend, must help me against that with your prayers. In so far as she accuses me of "worldliness" she is right: but if by "earthiness" she means my tendency to "come down to brass tacks" and try to deal with the ordinary petty sins & virtues of secular & domestic life, she is wrong. That is a thing that ought to be done and has not yet been done enough.

The Collected Letters of C. S. Lewis, Volume III

WORRY

A great many people (not you) do now seem to think that the mere state of being worried is in itself meritorious. I don't think it is. We must, if it so happens, give our lives for others: but even while we're doing it, I think we're meant to enjoy Our Lord and, in Him, our friends, our food, our sleep, our jokes, and the birds' song and the frosty sunrise.

The Collected Letters of C. S. Lewis, Volume II

Remember one is given strength to bear what happens to one, but not the 100 and 1 different things that might happen. And don't say God has proved that He can make you fear poverty, illness, etc. I am sure God never teaches us the fear of anything but Himself.

The Collected Letters of C. S. Lewis, Volume III

WORSHIP

He demands our worship, our obedience, our prostration. Do we suppose that they can do Him any good, or fear, like the chorus in Milton, that human irreverence can bring about "His glory's diminution"? A man can no more diminish God's glory by refusing to worship Him than a lunatic can put out the sun by scribbling the word "darkness" on the walls of his cell. But God wills our good, and our good is to love Him (with that responsive love proper to creatures) and to love Him we must know Him: and if we know Him, we shall in fact fall on our faces. If we do not, that only shows that what we are trying to love is not yet God—though it may be the nearest approximation to God which our thought and fantasy can attain.

The Problem of Pain

One thing seems certain. It is no good angling for the rich moments. God sometimes seems to speak to us most intimately when He catches us, as it were, off our guard. Our preparations to receive Him sometimes have the opposite effect. Doesn't Charles Williams say somewhere that "the altar must often be built in one place in order that the fire from heaven may descend somewhere else"?

Letters to Malcolm: Chiefly on Prayer

It is in the process of being worshipped that God communicates His presence to men.

Reflections on the Psalms

WRITING

No, one can't put these experiences into words: though all writing is a continual attempt to do so. Indeed, in a sense, one can hardly put anything into words: only the simplest colours have names, and hardly any of the smells. The simple physical pains and (still more) the pleasures can't be expressed in language. I labour the point lest the devil shd. hereafter try to make you believe that what was wordless was therefore vague and nebulous. But in reality it is just the clearest, the most concrete, and the most indubitable realities which escape language: not because they are vague but because language is. What goes easily into words is precisely the abstract—thought about "matter" (not apples or snuff), about "population" (not actual babies), and so on. Poetry I take to be the continual effort to bring language back to the actual.

The Collected Letters of C. S. Lewis, Volume II

What really matters is:

1. Always try to use the language so as to make quite clear what you mean and make sure yr. sentence couldn't mean anything else.

2. Always prefer the plain direct word to the long, vague one. Don't implement promises, but keep them.

3. Never use abstract nouns when concrete ones will do. If you mean "more people died" don't say "mortality rose."

4. In writing. Don't use adjectives which merely tell us how you want us to feel about the thing you are describing. I mean, instead

of telling us a thing was "terrible," describe it so that we'll be terrified. Don't say it was "delightful": make us say "delightful" when we've read the description. You see, all those words (horrifying, wonderful, hideous, exquisite) are only like saying to your readers "Please will you do my job for me."

5. Don't use words too big for the subject. Don't say "infinitely" when you mean "very": otherwise you'll have no word left when you want to talk about something really infinite.

The Collected Letters of C .S. Lewis, Volume II

It is very hard to give any general advice about writing. Here's my attempt.

1) Turn off the Radio.

2) Read all the good books you can, and avoid nearly all magazines.

3) Always write (and read) with the ear, not the eye. You shd. hear every sentence you write as if it was being read aloud or spoken. If it does not sound nice, try again.

4) Write about what really interests you, whether it is real things or imaginary things, and nothing else. (Notice this means that if you are interested only in writing you will never be a writer, because you will have nothing to write about . . .)

5) Take great pains to be clear. Remember that though you start by knowing what you mean, the reader doesn't, and a single ill-chosen word may lead him to a total misunderstanding. In a story it is terribly easy just to forget that you have not told the reader something that he wants to know—the whole picture is so clear in your own mind that you forget that it isn't the same in his.

6) When you give up a bit of work don't (unless it is hopelessly bad) throw it away. Put it in a drawer. It may come in useful later. Much of my best work, or what I think my best, is the rewriting of things begun and abandoned years earlier.

7) Don't use a typewriter. The noise will destroy your sense of rhythm, which still needs years of training.

8) Be sure you know the meaning (or meanings) of every word you use.

The Collected Letters of C. S. Lewis, Volume III

The way for a person to develop a style is (a) to know exactly what he wants to say, and (b) to be sure he is saying exactly that. The reader, we must remember, does not start by knowing what we mean. If our words are ambiguous, our meaning will escape him. I sometimes think that writing is like driving sheep down a road. If there is any gate open to the left or the right the readers will most certainly go into it.

God in the Dock

ZEAL

There can be intemperance in work just as in drink. What feels like zeal may be only fidgets or even the flattering of one's self-importance. As MacDonald says "In holy things may be unholy greed." And by doing what "one's station and its duties" does not demand, one can make oneself less fit for the duties it does demand, and so commit some injustice. Just you give Mary a little chance as well as Martha!

The Collected Letters of C. S. Lewis, Volume III

We can become scrupulous or fanatical; we can, in what seems zeal but is really presumption, embrace tasks never intended for us. That is the truth in the temptation.

The Weight of Glory

BIBLIOGRAPHY

BOOKS BY C. S. LEWIS

The Abolition of Man: Or Reflections on Education with Special Reference to the Teaching of English in the Upper Forms of Schools. Riddell Memorial Lectures, fifteenth series. London: Oxford Univ. Press, 1943. London: Bles, Centenary Press, 1946. New York: Macmillan, 1947. Newly reset edition: San Francisco: HarperSanFrancisco, 2001.

Arthurian Torso. In *Taliesin Through Logres, The Region of the Summer Stars,* and *Arthurian Torso.* One-volume edition. Introduction by Mary McDermott Shideler. Grand Rapids, MI: Eerdmans, 1974.

C. S. Lewis: Essay Collection and Other Short Pieces. Edited by Lesley Walmsley. London: HarperCollins, 2000.

C. S. Lewis: Letters to Children. Edited by Lyle W. Dorsett and Marjorie Lamp Mead. Foreword by Douglas H. Gresham. New York: Macmillan, 1985.

C. S. Lewis on Stories: And Other Essays on Literature. Edited by Walter Hooper. New York: Harcourt Brace Jovanovich, 1982.

Christian Reflections. Edited with a preface by Walter Hooper. London: Chapman, 1967. Grand Rapids, MI: Eerdmans, 1967.

The Collected Letters of C. S. Lewis, Volume I: Family Letters, 1905–1931. Edited by Walter Hooper. London and New York: HarperCollins, 2000.

The Collected Letters of C. S. Lewis, Volume II: Books, Broadcasts and the War 1931–1949. Edited by Walter Hooper. London and New York: HarperCollins, 2004.

The Collected Letters of C. S. Lewis, Volume III: Narnia, Cambridge, and Joy, 1950–1963. Edited by Walter Hooper. London and New York: HarperCollins, 2006.

The Collected Poems of C. S. Lewis. Edited by Walter Hooper. London: HarperCollins, 1994.

English Literature in the Sixteenth Century Excluding Drama. The Completion of "The Clark Lectures," Trinity College, Cambridge, 1944. *The Oxford History of English Literature,* vol. 3. Oxford: Clarendon, 1954; abridged paperback edition, 1973.

An Experiment in Criticism. Cambridge: Cambridge Univ. Press, 1961.

The Four Loves. London: Bles, 1960. New York: Harcourt, Brace & World, 1960.

God in the Dock: Essays on Theology and Ethics. Edited by Walter Hooper. Grand Rapids, MI: Eerdmans, 1970.

The Great Divorce: A Dream. London: Bles, Centenary Press, 1945. New York: Macmillan, 1946. Newly reset edition: San Francisco: HarperSanFrancisco, 2001.

A Grief Observed. London: Faber, 1961 (under the pseudonym of N. W. Clerk). Reprinted, as by C. S. Lewis, 1964, Greenwich, CT: Seabury, 1963. Newly reset edition: San Francisco: HarperSanFrancisco, 2001.

The Horse and His Boy. London: Bles, 1954. New York: Macmillan, 1954. Entirely reset world edition: HarperCollins, 1994.

In Our Tongues. Edited by James Patrick Stevenson. London: Society for Promoting Christian Knowledge, 1944.

The Last Battle: A Story for Children. London: John Lane, the Bodley Head, 1956. Without subtitle, New York: Macmillan, 1956. Entirely reset world edition: HarperCollins, 1994.

Letters to Malcolm: Chiefly on Prayer. London: Bles, 1964. New York: Harcourt, Brace & World, 1964.

The Lion, the Witch and the Wardrobe: A Story for Children. London: Bles, 1950. New York: Macmillan, 1950. Entirely reset world edition: HarperCollins, 1994.

The Magician's Nephew. London: Bodley Head, 1955. New York: Macmillan, 1955. Entirely reset world edition: HarperCollins, 1994.

Mere Christianity, a revised and amplified edition, with a new introduction, of the three books *Broadcast Talks, Christian Behavior,* and *Beyond Personality*. London: Bles, 1952. As *Mere Christianity*, a revised and enlarged edition, with a new introduction, of the three books *The Case for Christianity, Christian Behavior,* and *Beyond Personality*. New York: Macmillan, 1952. Newly reset edition: San Francisco: HarperSanFrancisco, 2001.

Miracles: A Preliminary Study. London, Bles, 1947. New York: Macmillan, 1947. With revision of Chapter 3, London: Collins, 1960. New York: Macmillan, 1978. Newly reset edition: San Francisco: HarperSanFrancisco, 2001.

Perelandra. London: John Lane, the Bodley Head, 1943. New York: Macmillan, 1944; Scribner Classics edition, 1999.

The Personal Heresy: A Controversy. E. M. W. Tillyard and C. S. Lewis. London: Oxford Univ. Press, 1939.

The Pilgrim's Regress: An Allegorical Apology for Christianity, Reason and Romanticism. London: Dent, 1933. New edition with preface, footnotes and running headlines: London: Sheed and Ward, 1944. Grand Rapids, MI: Eerdmans, 1958.

A Preface to Paradise Lost. Oxford: Oxford Univ. Press, 1942.

Present Concerns. Edited by Walter Hooper. New York: Harcourt Brace Jovanovich, 1986.

Prince Caspian: The Return to Narnia. London: Bles, 1951. New York: Macmillan, 1951. Entirely reset world edition: HarperCollins, 1994.

The Problem of Pain. London: Centenary, 1940. New York: Macmillan, 1943. Newly reset edition: San Francisco: HarperSanFrancisco, 2001.

Reflections on the Psalms. London: Bles, 1958. New York: Harcourt, Brace & World, 1958.

Rehabilitations and Other Essays. London: Oxford Univ. Press, 1939.

The Screwtape Letters. London: Bles, 1942. New York: Macmillan, 1943. With a new Screwtape letter as *The Screwtape Letters and Screwtape Proposes a Toast,* with a new and additional preface: London: Bles, 1961. New York: Macmillan, 1962. Newly reset edition: San Francisco: HarperSanFrancisco, 2001.

Selected Literary Essays. Edited by Walter Hooper. Cambridge: Cambridge Univ. Press, 1969.

The Silver Chair. London: Bles, 1953; New York: Macmillan, 1953. Reprint edition: HarperTrophy, 1944

Studies in Medieval and Renaissance Literature. Collected by Walter Hooper. Cambridge: Cambridge Univ. Press, 1966.

Studies in Words. Cambridge: Cambridge Univ. Press, 1960.

Surprised by Joy: The Shape of My Early Life. London: Bles, 1955. New York: Harcourt, Brace & World, 1956.

That Hideous Strength: A Modern Fairy-tale for Grown-ups. London: John Lane, the Bodley Head, 1945. New York: Macmillan, 1946; Scribner Classics edition, 1999.

Till We Have Faces: A Myth Retold. London: Bles, 1956. New York: Harcourt, Brace & World, 1957.

The Voyage of the DAWN TREADER. London, Bles, 1952. New York: Macmillan, 1952. Entirely reset world edition: HarperCollins, 1994.

The Weight of Glory: And Other Addresses. New York: Macmillan, 1949. Revised and expanded edition, edited and with an introduction by Walter Hooper. New York: Macmillan, 1980. Newly reset edition: San Francisco: HarperSanFrancisco, 2001.

The World's Last Night: And Other Essays. New York: Harcourt, Brace, 1960.

OTHER SOURCES

Como, James T., ed. *C. S. Lewis at the Breakfast Table and Other Reminiscences.* New York: Macmillan, 1979.

Davidman, Joy. *Smoke on the Mountain: An Interpretation of the Ten Commandments.* Philadelphia: Westminster, 1954.

Essays Presented to Charles Williams. Edited by C. S. Lewis. London: Oxford Univ. Press, 1947. Grand Rapids, MI: Eerdmans, 1966.

George MacDonald: An Anthology. Edited with a preface by C. S. Lewis. London: Bles, 1946. New York: Macmillan, 1947. Newly reset edition: San Francisco: HarperSanFrancisco, 2001.

PERMISSIONS

C. S. LEWIS
THEMATIC INDEX